Born in Jarrow, brought up in Hull, and trained as an architect in Newcastle, Alan Plater has been a full-time writer since 1961, with almost three hundred assorted credits in radio, television, theatre and films – plus six novels, occasional journalism, broadcasting and teaching.

His first plays were written for radio, a medium he still loves. *The Journal of Vasilije Bogdanovic* won the inaugural 1983 Sony Radio Award. His television career began with a string of single plays as well as contributions to the pioneering *Z Cars* series. Subsequent work has included *Barchester Chronicles*, *The Beiderbecke Trilogy*, *Fortunes of War*, *A Very British Coup*, *Misterioso*, *Doggin' Around*, *The Last of the Blonde Bombshells*, *Belonging* and, most recently, *The Last Will and Testament of Billy Two-Sheds*.

He has won Awards from, among others, BAFTA, the Broadcasting Press Guild and the Royal Television Society – plus an International Emmy (USA), the Golden Fleece of Georgia (CIS), the Grand Prix of the Banff Festival (Canada) and the Screenwriting Award of the Biarritz Festival. A third generation trade unionist, he was President of the Writers' Guild from 1991 to 1995. In 2005 he won BAFTA's much-cherished Dennis Potter Award and was given a CBE in the New Year Honours List.

He lives very contentedly in London with his wife, Shirley. When he remembers where he left his spare time, he spends it adoring his grandchildren, hanging around Ronnie Scott's and worrying about Hull City.

D0870114

ALAN PLATER

Doggin' Around

illustrated by the author

Published by Northway Publications
39 Tytherton Road, London N19 4PZ, UK.
www.northwaybooks.com

Copyright © Alan Plater 2006

Alan Plater has asserted his right to be identified as author of this work
in accordance with the Copyright, Designs and Patents Act 1988.

All rights whatsoever in this work are strictly reserved and application
for any other use including mechanical recording of any kind shall be
made to Alexandra Cann Representation, 12 Abingdon Road, London
W8 6AF, email: mail@alexandracann.co.uk and to the publishers. No
part of this book may be circulated in any form of binding or cover other
than that in which it is published and without a similar condition including this condition being imposed on the subsequent purchaser.

The publishers acknowledge with thanks the kind permission of Mark
Herman to reprint the front cover illustration and the *Independent* to
reprint the back cover colour portrait photo by Mark Chilvers.

A CIP record for this book is available from the British Library.

ISBN 0 9550908 0 6

First published 2006.

Printed and bound in Great Britain by Bookmarque Ltd, Croydon,
Surrey.

For Marie – my first music teacher

Contents

1.

Schooldays

In 1999 I wrote a letter to Duke Ellington. Since he died in 1974, it might suggest I was a little slow on the uptake. Not so. The letter was part of a radio series in which people were invited to write letters to icons of their choice. The series was called, appropriately enough, *Letter to an Icon*. I chose The Duke. The novelist Stan Barstow, an old comrade from the Northern mafia-in-exile, chose J. B. Priestley, and we recorded our pieces on the same day in Manchester, thus paving the way for a lovely pissy supper afterwards. We compared notes on the way the world was going to hell and was only likely to be redeemed by people like Jack Priestley, The Duke and, of course, ourselves.

Here, with a few tweaks, is what I said to my hero:

Dear Duke Ellington,

As I write this letter, there's a record playing. Not a CD, but a long-playing record. I bought it new from a shop in 1954 and now it's a little worn and scratchy. That should tell you I am of a certain age – indeed, I too am a little worn and scratchy.

But there's more. It's the first record I ever bought. At the time I was a student of architecture, and by a careful juggling of my grant, vacation work for the Post Office and British Railways and early experiments with a bank overdraft, I was able to buy an occasional record. And this was the very first. It's called *Ellington Masterpieces* (Columbia sx 1022). You probably remember it. It has your photograph on the sleeve.

The tune is called 'Mood Indigo' but you'd know that, since you wrote it – in 1931 according to my big book of famous tunes. It's the first piece of your music I ever heard – on my grandparents' wireless set during the war. I must have been about five years old. Something about it made my ears tingle.

For a start it had so few notes. Most tunes had hundreds of notes but this one only had three or four. These days it's called minimalism though I fancy it's something to do with genius.

I left architecture behind in the fifties as a favour to the environment. Since then I've made a living writing plays, and the greatest line in drama runs 'To be or not to be' – five two-letter words, one three-letter word. Call it minimalism, call it genius – either way, you and William Shakespeare were both very good at it.

Now let's make a leap – of what? Can it really be over four decades? From that little kid in a house in Jarrow-on-Tyne to what we might recklessly call the grown-up human being who's writing to you now. Over those years I've listened to hours of your music and read most of what's been written about you. I've even contributed myself. Your entry in at least one *Encyclopaedia of Popular Music* bears my name.

You may well have mixed feelings about this. You once said, famously, 'too much talk stinks up the place' – though it's never as simple as that, especially with music which, as a rule, can be described but not explained. You can write down the notes of 'Mood Indigo' on a piece of manuscript paper but you can't explain why the tune climbed inside the head of a five-year-old kid in Jarrow, in the industrial North of England, over half-a-century ago and refused ever to move out. And yet... maybe you can... here's what you said about it:

'"Mood Indigo"... it's just a story about a little girl and a little boy. They are about eight and the girl loves the boy. They never speak of it, of course, but she just likes the way he wears his hat. Every day he comes to her house at a certain time and she sits in her window and waits. Then one day he doesn't come. "Mood Indigo" just tells how she feels.'

Well, it may be true that the wrong sort of talk – let's say by well-meaning critics and maybe people like me – does have the capacity to stink up the place, but in your case you write a good tune and sure as hell you talk a good one. Indeed, if dictionaries of quotations cast their net wider than Oxbridge, you'd have several pages to yourself.

For example, when your work was plagiarised, as happened on several occasions, you said: 'They must be good tunes if so many people want to steal them.' And a musician friend in Montreal, Canada, told me, years ago, that you summoned him to a meeting in your hotel room where you greeted him, fresh from the shower, stark naked, with the words: 'Ah, Ronald, you've caught me with my charisma showing.'

One of my favourites dates back to the 1950s when, on a tour of the United Kingdom, you met the Queen who said to you, after the time-honoured royal fashion: 'When were you last in England, Mr Ellington?' To which you replied: 'In 1933, Your Majesty – years before you were born.' Later you wrote a tune for the Queen called 'Single Petal of a Rose'.

That, I have to tell you, is style – as if you didn't know. Its function, and its effect, is to make the person you are speaking to think that he or she is the most important person in the cosmos. Even if it involves bending or even abandoning the truth – an idea I'll get back to later in the case of the black silk jacket.

Then, of course, there was the 'Love You Madly' routine. At the end of your concerts you would address the audience thus:

'You're very beautiful, very gracious, very talented and we'd like you to know that we do love you madly.'

Professional writers hate to admit they've ever been influenced by anybody, but in your case I happily make an exception. You have had a direct influence on me, not on my work but on what these days are called my social skills.

It began with the arrival on the scene of answering machines and those voices saying: 'I'm sorry, we can't get to the phone right now, but if you'd like to leave a message, we'll call you back as soon as possible.'

I don't know whether these things had taken over the earth at the time of your death in 1974 but the place is overflowing with them now, to the extent that some people apologise for being at home at all to answer their own telephones, when they should be out getting rich or famous.

In the beginning I refused to speak to answering machines. I'd simply hang up. Then we all began to learn answering machine technique, and the one I developed went roughly like this:

'Hi, it's Alan speaking. Perhaps you'd like to call me back. For the moment, Shirley and I would simply like you to know that you're very beautiful, very gracious, very talented and we do love you madly.'

Of course, we didn't do this indiscriminately – only with recognisably human beings – never with agents of global corporations or the state apparatus. The result was that people always returned the phone calls. And on more than one occasion the caller admitted that he or she had had a really lousy day and our message had gone some way towards delousing their universe. So far so good.

Another item in your repertoire was the re-invented childhood. You told audiences how, as a child in Washington, you were taught to play piano by a music teacher called Mrs Clinkscales and, at your first lesson, she said to you: 'Edward, whatever you do, never share a platform with Oscar Peterson.'

Now any jazz fan would know that when you were a kid Oscar Peterson wasn't yet born. That was the joke. But only an obsessive like me would take the principle of that joke and recycle it into his own life. Perhaps the best example was a year or two back when I was at a writers' meeting. I was wearing a silk jacket, though not as fancy as the sort that you wore. It was just a black, off-the-peg, lumberjacket affair from the same people who mass-produce my underpants. During the coffee break, a woman colleague stroked the jacket appreciatively and said: 'That's lovely to touch.'

Without thinking I said: 'Well, when I was a young lad in the Industrial North, my Dad used to say to me: "Whatever you do in life, son, always make sure you're tactile."' This was, and is, a pack of lies. For a start, my Dad was a Geordie and not a Yorkshireman, and he would never have said anything as dumb as that. But I think the woman believed me.

I now call this Clinkscales Syndrome. Making up totally ludicrous stories about childhood and seeing whether I can make people believe them. Indeed, I have a whole fantasy childhood of this kind. I tell my grandchildren:

'Of course, there was no television in those days. We had to make our own entertainment. We'd take turns throwing stones at the lamplighter and on Sunday nights we'd have musical evenings. We'd all gather round the piano in the front room and chop it up for firewood.'

My grandchildren, who are the smartest people I know, don't believe a word of it. But they come out smiling which is, of course, the heart of the matter.

Whichever way you hold it up to the light, this is a thank you letter. For the music, obviously. But also for being around in the twentieth century, and for dedicating your life to making people feel better, whether they were kings, queens or commoners. This is no small achievement for a black kid from Washington, D.C. In a racist society, you took your pain and made it beautiful – and you took your joy and made it transcendent.

This year, 1999, we've been celebrating your centenary with concerts and radio programmes and articles in the glossy magazines. There's been a lot of talk stinking the place up but mostly we've listened to the music: the sacred and the profane, the sweet and the sad, the swinging and the reflective.

It's all of a piece – just something in the way you wore your life. Those of us who have heard the blues at midnight would like to remind you that you remain very handsome, very gracious, very talented, very generous and we do love you madly.

* * *

I wrote that letter six years ago and, looking at it now, it's a relief to realise that I still agree with most of it, though I forgot to tell him about our dog, a handsome, brave, big-hearted Irish setter called The Duke. We loved him madly, that being the only way you can love an Irish setter, and miss him still, walking carefully around the space where he used to lie, at the foot of the bed. Reason and logic have no part in the philosophy of Irish setters, nor in the love they inspire in their owners.

THE DUKE (d. 1992)

The only thing I query in the letter – and I probably put it in for dramatic effect, dramatic effect being what I do for a living – is the claim that 'Mood Indigo' is the first piece of music I ever heard. Can that be true? It's doubtful.

My parents' generation was almost certainly the last to regard a musical evening as a normal part of family life in urban England. We would gather, notably at holiday times, in my grandparents' front room for a sing-song. My Auntie May played the piano, my Uncle Harry played a one-string fiddle, which he'd made out of an old cigar box (I still have it on a shelf in the study) and my dad was a keen amateur baritone who had sung in a local concert party and in Gilbert and Sullivan. Later, after we started piano lessons, my sister Marie and I would do our party pieces – and whatever the music, everybody joined in. Consequently there's a songbook at the back of my head with a repertoire that's at least a hundred years old. Songs like 'The Lost Chord' and 'Bless This House' still cause a frisson if I hear them, and I know the words of dozens of old music-hall songs without having learned them. They're just stuck there, in the subconscious; but they don't haunt me, the way 'Mood Indigo' did from that first hearing.

I also fell in love with bands at an early age. The family moved from Jarrow to Hull in 1938 and in that immediate pre-war period we would go to the Palace, a number one variety theatre. One of the acts we saw was Harry Roy and his band, at a time when band-leaders were the rock stars of the day.

I can't remember anything they played but if I close my eyes I can see them in their glitzy finery with their dapper leader out front, looking like a cross between Cab Calloway and Max Miller.

Later, during the war, a touring show called *Wings* came to the New Theatre in Hull. Produced by Ralph Reader of Scout *Gang Show* fame, the only thing I remember was the band, which must have been the famous RAF Dance Band that was later transformed into the Squadronnaires. It's even possible – though impossible to verify – that Kenny Baker, with whom I was to have a memorable grown-up association, was onstage that night. My parents told me that the band was the only bit of the show I apparently liked.

Though they had nothing to do with jazz, I have special memories of the cowboy band, Big Bill Campbell and his Rocky Mountain Rhythm because this is the only other band that I remember seeing – at the Tivoli Theatre in Hull when I was about seven years old. It was special because it was the first time I challenged (strictly inside my head, which is where I lived a lot of the time) what I saw on the stage.

As I remember, the musicians were all dressed in cowboy clothes and Campbell stood out front, dressed in even smarter cowboy clothes. The clothes were a bit frillier than I'd expected. The musicians were all very bronzed, unnaturally so in Hull where most people got rusty if they got anything.

For five minutes I was deeply impressed. But even at that age I was a smart-arse because I could read and literacy is where smart-arsery begins. I knew they were playing twice-nightly variety that week and I knew they'd be going on to do the same in Leeds or Sheffield. Five minutes into the act I was struck by an obvious thought: who is looking after the cows?

Other thoughts followed. If they bring the cows with them, where are they now? And how do the cowboys keep their clothes so clean? And don't those frills get in the way when they're rounding up the herd? And if the cows are at home, why are they in the rocky mountains?

My logic was impeccable. Roy Rogers was my favourite film star and I knew, from his films, that cows lived on plains, not on rocky mountains. If they lived on rocky mountains if would be impossible to round them up and stampedes would be out of the question. There was no doubt about it. Cows lived on plains and goats lived on rocky mountains. But I suppose Big Bill Campbell and his

Rocky Mountain Goat-herds wouldn't have looked so good on the posters.

Woven into those years of perplexity were the piano lessons. For about a year I went every Thursday to a teacher along the road but had already decided that I would rather play football than music. Part of the problem was the duff music I was expected to practise – what seemed to me, even then, naff little tunes with wet titles like the 'Fairy Waltz' and the 'Buttercup March'. My sister, who hung in and plays exceedingly well to this day, tried to overcome the problem by buying me a simple piano transcription of Mel Powell's 'My Guy's Come Back' – a tactic which rebounded, since after a while it was the only piece I would ever play. It's a simple little number, magical when played by Mel Powell's Uptown Hall Gang, but less entrancing hammered out unrelentingly by a truculent eight-year-old, who'd rather be kicking a ball about in the park.

When my mother suggested, gently as was her way, that I should stop the lessons, thus saving half-a-crown a week on the family budget, I leapt at the chance, to great relief all round. Even the piano seemed to smile. These days I can't even play 'My Guy's Come Back' but retain enough rudimentary knowledge to have more-or-less sensible conversations with musicians when collaborating on musical projects.

This once helped me win an argument with the great jazz pianist, Colin Purbrook, about how many bars there were in Duke Ellington's 'Blues I Love to Sing', though it should be reported that Colin's way of arguing was to raise one eyebrow a fraction of a centimeter.

I'd set some lyrics to the tune for a stage show called *Rent Party* produced at the Theatre Royal, Stratford East in 1988. Colin, who was our musical director, looked at the lyrics.

'You've written too many words,' he said.

'No I haven't. It's a forty-eight bar tune.'

'Is it?' he said, and checked the sheet music. 'So it is. How did you know?'

'I listened to it on the record and counted them,' I told him, trying not to smirk. So the music lessons weren't a total waste of time.

As I drifted into my teens, jazz and swing took a serious grip on my imagination, courtesy of the wireless. There was BBC *Jazz Club* to listen to on a Saturday evening, after getting home from the football match, and Jack Jackson would sometimes sneak a Stan Kenton record onto his late night record show. There were also regular broadcasts by the top big bands of the day. The first time I heard 'Cottontail' it was played by Geraldo's orchestra, of all people, on his weekly programme, and the fact that I remember this says it all about the growth of my obsession.

Like many fans before and since, I often had to defend my position. Every Friday night, four of my dad's mates would come to our house to play snooker on our half-size table. It was a tradition going back to the war when whoever wasn't playing in the doubles' game would be outside on firewatch duty. During the war, their wives would be next door, knitting pullovers and socks for our gallant Russian allies. In peacetime they would go to the theatre.

Around ten o'clock on a Friday night there was usually a band on the wireless and I would turn it up as loudly as I dared. On the night in question I was listening to one of the more jazz-oriented outfits – possibly Harry Gold or Freddie Randall.

Mr Jervis, the man from next door, an ex-trawlerman who'd bought himself into a fish-merchant business following a win on the Irish Sweep and who loved winding me up, looked at me.

'What's that row, Alan?'

'Jazz.'

'Is it good?'

'Yes.'

'What makes it good?'

It was a hell of a question, but I was up to it.

'It's expressive.'

'What is it expressing?'

That was an even better question and I couldn't answer it. I probably went into an early adolescent sulk. Sulking became something of a speciality through my teens. The *Picture Post* ran an article about the young tearaways on the London jazz scene and there was a photograph of Humphrey Lyttelton complete with long sideboards. That was it. I cultivated long sideboards as an act of homage, combined with a centre-parting inspired by an brilliantly eccentric Irish centre-half called Gerry Bowler who played briefly for Hull City, before they decided Celtic extravagance wasn't the best form of defence. I ended up looking like an apprentice croupier in a struggling casino. All is vanity, saith the preacher, and it peaks in adolescence.

The first time I ever heard live jazz was, of all places, in a youth club. The fact is, youth clubs played a very small part in my adolescence. The sound of table tennis was a little strident for my taste – snooker was and is much more soothing – and the smell of prayer-books oppressive. Indeed, I only once set foot inside a youth club and that was around 1951, to hear a performance by the splendidly named Port of Hull Jazz Band.

I'm pretty sure that the whole thing was dressed up as education, perhaps to reassure the vicar, and one of the musicians gave us a carefully-edited potted history of New Orleans jazz between the tunes.

I don't remember much. Nobody had told me you were supposed to keep careful note of the personnel for posterity, though I recall a tuba player and a clarinettist who looked a bit like Pee Wee Russell. I assume the resemblance was deliberate, and I obviously understood the role model stuff – hence the sideboards and centre-parting – though we didn't call it that.

Through my teens I wanted to be lots of people. They included James Thurber, Saul Steinberg, Dylan Thomas and Raich Carter, soon to be joined by Duke Ellington, Django Reinhardt and Charlie Christian. The thought of becoming

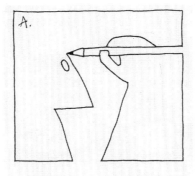

TRYING TO BE SAUL STEINBERG

a playwright had never occurred to me: if you'd suggested Arthur Miller or Tennessee Williams as fantasy possibilities I'd have regarded it as terminal daftness.

Then Les entered my life. When you're in your teens, it's important that among your mates there should be somebody like Les: a sort of equal and opposite lunatic.

When he was sixteen, Les had one obsession: collecting

musical instruments. He bought them from second-hand shops. He did weekend work, so he could afford to pay as much as seven-and-six (38p) for some of them. At his peak, he had three violins, a trombone without a mouthpiece, a clarinet without a reed, a banjo with never more than three strings, his parents' piano, a zither and the school's double bass.

The point about this collection was that he couldn't actually play any of them, except the double bass, which he could play slightly. Slightly was good enough to get him into our school orchestra. It wasn't the greatest school orchestra in the history of music but it was the best one in the school. Les played a few undemanding notes, very low down, and mostly they passed unnoticed beneath the sound of the violin section. If kids played anything in those days, it tended to be the piano or the violin, though we did have a reluctant bugler called Stuart who was wheeled out every November 11th to play the 'Last Post' in our school assembly.

Les became obsessed with the need to get the double bass home, to form part of his collection. He got permission from the music teacher to take it home to practise on. This would have been perfectly reasonable except that he lived about three miles from school and travelled on his bike. Any normal double bass player – though that may be a contradiction in terms – will tell you it's not an easy instrument to carry on a bike.

But Les was more than equal to the task. He was one of five children and, aside from the biggest frying pan I've ever seen, there were a few spare prams in the house. These were proper perambulators, unlike the plastic sachets or rucksacks used to transport kids today. Les dismantled one of the prams and used the wheels to make a small trolley which enabled him to tow the double bass behind his bike.

Les also taught me that life only got interesting after midnight. I'd go down to his house and we'd sit in the room full of instruments, listening in the wee small hours to Radio Luxembourg and the American Forces Network. We'd take turns joining in with the music on the double bass.

We were doomed. I was more doomed than he was, but I didn't realise it at the time, though he was the one who fell off his bike late one night while towing the double bass around a major traffic roundabout. This was about the time we had discovered the joys of bottled beer. The double bass collided with a Keep Left sign and ended up with five sound-holes instead of two. Les insisted it gave the music additional resonance but always regretted the police weren't around as he always fancied being up in court for being drunk in charge of a double bass. This was partly because we once worked for a drunken farmer called Major Burke who had told us that during the war in the Western Desert, he had presided over the courtmartial of a soldier charged with being drunk in charge of a camel. We were easily influenced by romantic tales of that kind.

As we were leaving school one day, Les said to me: 'You've got to come round tonight. I've got something to show you.' There might have been excitement in his eyes but it was difficult to tell because he wore traditional style National Health spectacles which he was always breaking when playing football – in football as in politics he was an erratic and aggressive left-winger – and he always fixed them himself with insulating tape, elastoplast and blind faith. There was very little of the original spectacles left, apart from the lenses.

When I arrived at the house, that evening, he showed me

his surprise. He had bought a zither from a second-hand shop. It must have been the only second-hand zither in the whole of Yorkshire. It and Les were made for each other.

The zither was quite a fashionable instrument following the release of the film *The Third Man* in 1949, which had as one of its star attractions the theme music played by Anton Karas who, according to film legend, had been heard playing by the director Carol Reed in a bar in Vienna. The tune made the charts and drove everyone crazy for several weeks.

According to the *Oxford Companion to Music* a zither has a flat soundboard with four or five melody strings – to play the tune – and thirty-seven accompanying strings – to play the oompah bits. The one Les had bought looked like the real article.

I did the unforgivable thing.

'Give us a tune,' I said.

Les gave me a pained look then ran his fingers across the strings. All the notes sounded identical.

'You can get that same effect strumming on our canary's cage,' I said.

'That's because it hasn't been tuned,' said Les.

'Is that why I'm here? We're going to spend an entire evening tuning a second-hand zither?'

'It won't cost you a penny. You got anything better to do?'

I hadn't.

The truly amazing part was that Les had found a library book with instructions on how to do it. He was the only person I have ever known who would go into a public library and demand, as a democratic right, a book on how to tune a zither. And he got one. It's a good test of any library.

We tuned all forty-one or forty-two strings. The mistake

might have been to tune it to the family piano which hadn't been tuned in living memory. Or maybe the library book was out of date. Or maybe it wasn't a zither at all, but a species of balalaika or bird-cage. After two hours of patient work we had snapped every string on the instrument.

Even Les agreed that buying zither strings might not be all that easy in Hull. So we put it in a corner with the trombone, the clarinet, the three violins and the school double bass and went out to do a little research into the subject of demure under-age drinking. Two halves of Hull Brewery bitter were the outer limit of our capacity and budget, but generally enabled us to address the world's problems and arrive at clear solutions by closing time.

Les wasn't the only disruptive element in my youth. My mate Barry was another though he didn't mean to be. Barry never meant to be anything or do anything. He was laidback way before the phrase had been invented. He was so laidback you could slide him under the door.

Barry was unusual among our gang because he'd left school at fifteen and got a job, with wages and a stamp card. He became a clerk at the Labour Exchange. They were fine places, old-fashioned Labour Exchanges. We used to go there in the holidays looking for casual work. There were separate entrances for clerical and manual workers, everything had been painted green a long time ago and there were always long queues.

It was also compulsory to smoke Woodbines if you were in the Labour Exchange. Dog ends littered the floor like the first snows of winter. Ash-trays had been invented but were regarded as cissy. They were macho times in the industrial North. Ash-trays at the Labour Exchange were as irrelevant as urinals at a Rugby League ground.

It was only after Barry started to work there that we

found out the reason for the long queues. The clerks used to have competitions, with modest side-bets, to see who could get the longest queue. Apparently it was the only way they could make the job interesting. I put this story into a television play back in the 1960s, when we still had television plays.

Barry, like most people with steady jobs, got his fun after hours. I'm pretty sure girls came into this – he had been one of the first kids in our class to start combing his hair regularly. And, crucially, he could play the piano. He never mentioned it while he was at school because he was terrified of being recruited for the school orchestra.

To be absolutely precise, he could play three-and-a-half tunes. They were Pinetop's 'Boogie Woogie', Stan Kenton's 'Intermission Riff', a Vic Lewis original called 'Music for Moderns', and part of 'The Man I Love'. He could play the main theme which is constructed on a simple series of descending chords, but he'd never got around to learning the middle eight.

I suspect Barry's philosophy was that three-and-a-half tunes were enough to attract the attention of girls, or as many as he needed on an average day. As far as I'm aware, it worked. But it's also clear that as a piano player he wasn't exactly dedicated.

I suggested to him he should learn the middle eight of 'The Man I Love'.

'Why?' he said.

'Then you could play it all the way through,' I said.

'I can play it all the way through,' he said, 'apart from the bit I leave out.'

Arguing with people from Hull is generally like that.

He also claimed that he *could* play twenty-four bars out of the thirty-two, which equalled three-quarters of the whole.

'That's seventy-five per cent of the whole tune,' he said. 'Seventy-five per cent will get you an honours degree when you go to university.'

'You can't play twenty-four bars,' I said, 'you can play the same eight bars over and over again and it's driving us barmy.'

In retrospect, this may seem like the most stupid and pointless argument in the history of human discourse, but we were sixteen years old. When you're sixteen, every argument is actually about the meaning of life.

For the record, most of our arguments ended the same way. One of the lads said 'Bollocks' and another one changed the subject. On this occasion, Les changed the subject. He said something very dangerous.

'We've got a piano player and a bass player,' he said then, looking at me: 'If you learned to play something, we could have a trio.'

Les, Barry and I agreed on a policy. We would form a trio modelled on that led by the great Nat King Cole. But we would only play jazz. We would never, under any circumstances, go commercial. Since nobody, under any circumstances, was likely to pay money to hear us, it was a purely ideological stance – a bit like being a socialist in Tony's Labour Party.

It was agreed that I should buy a guitar and learn to play it like the great Oscar Moore of the Nat Cole trio. I think we allowed a fortnight for this.

I went to Pat Cornell's music store on a street called Spring Bank in Hull. I had saved just over five pounds or, to be precise, I had saved about ninepence and my mother advanced me a fiver against Christmas and the next two birthdays.

The shop had two second-hand guitars in stock, one at five pounds and one at three. I asked about the cheaper of the two. If I bought that one, there'd be two quid left over for Woodbines and Hull Brewery bitter.

The man in the shop picked up the three pound guitar and brushed his fingers across the open strings.

'Nice resonant tone,' he said.

That was the moment to head for the door.

'It has been called the bargain of the month,' he added.

That was the moment to run away home as fast as my little legs would carry me. But we never do. I bought it together with an Ivor Mairants guitar tutor. I was so excited I got on the wrong bus to go home.

The principle of all stringed instruments is the same. You pluck the string and it emits a nice resonant tone, as demonstrated by the man in the shop. If you press the string down exactly halfway between the neck and the bridge, the note is exactly one octave higher.

But the people who make guitars obviously regard prospective players as idiots, and therefore they provide frets – bits of metal to tell you where to put your fingers – though it's obviously beyond any manufacturer's ability to indicate which are the white notes and which are the black.

What became clear, after much study of the instruction book, was that my three quid guitar had, some time in its history, been in an accident. Maybe Les given it a lift along with the school's double bass. The bridge had come adrift and had been put back in the wrong place.

The result was that if I put my fingers on the frets exact-ly as instructed, I had the only guitar in the world that was one note short of an octave. No wonder it was the bargain of the month.

The solution – which took much longer than tuning the zither – was to remove the strings, remove the bridge, put it back in the proper place, replace and retune the strings. It took a long time. It's probably the reason I failed A Level French.

I learned to play the chords of 'Pinetop's Boogie Woogie', 'Intermission Riff', 'Music for Moderns' and eight bars of 'The Man I Love'. Les towed the school double bass to our house and we rehearsed in our front room. We looked intense and smoked Woodbines.

'Do I sound like Oscar Moore?' I said to Les.

'It was better before you repaired it,' he said.

'It sounds a bit like a cheese grater,' said Barry. 'Mind you, I quite like the sound of a cheese grater.'

'Bollocks,' I said.

Then we noticed there were some girls staring in at the window. We stopped arguing and started playing, with even greater intensity. This was it. This was why young men became musicians and went into bands. We were a long way from Jerusalem but we'd caught our first glimpse of the suburbs.

We fed our fantasies by going to Sunday night jazz concerts at the City Hall. They were always packed. Fourteen hundred young people would demonstrate their non-conformity by stamping their feet in unison to the Humphrey Lyttelton band and yelling 'Onions!' at the right moment. We would shout our demands that they play 'The Saints' as an encore as if we were the first people in the history of the universe ever to have the idea. One of the lads claimed to have seen Johnny Parker, Humph's pianist, in a pub before one of the concerts, complaining bitterly that he'd come sixth in a *Melody Maker* poll won by Winifred Atwell.

Amazingly, Humph was the cutting edge of what we heard, but we'd settle for anything: Sid Phillips with his highly manicured dixieland, featuring Denny Dennis ('Britain's Bing Crosby'), was a regular visitor and modern jazz was represented by the Ray Ellington Quartet and, at the time in question, nobody else. We were particularly impressed by Ellington's suits. The only other hint of bebop was when Ted Heath featured a 'band within the band' and a handful of the guys would put on dark glasses to play 'Move'.

This was to influence our trio when we made our one public appearance. It was at a Sixth Form concert in 1952. Even in those days you could get away with murder if it was for charity. Our school was always raising money for good causes to enhance the quality of our education. First was the grand piano, then the double bass and then the observatory. Our headmaster was an astronomer of some distinction, well respected in the galaxy, and some of the more robust B-stream lads had built an observatory on the playing field – the girls' playing field, naturally. It wasn't as big as Jodrell Bank but more like a large brick igloo, surmounted with a dome made under the direction of the woodwork teacher.

Unfortunately the dome blew off during the first serious gale of the winter season and our 1952 charity concert was to raise money to pay for a new dome and maybe some better advice on how to fasten it down.

The show went on for hours. It was longer than Wagner's *Ring Cycle* but without the laughs. I had written some sketches and had the first, formative experience of hearing brilliant jokes and coruscating satire received by six

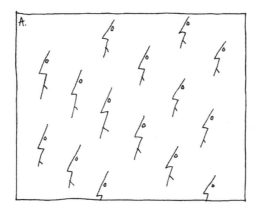

THE SILENCE OF AN AUDIENCE

hundred people in total silence. It was good practice for later life. A kid called Mike did a Mario Lanza impersonation. Another kid called Pete did an interminable magic act, most of which involved making things disappear. There were ribald requests from the back row that he should make himself disappear. In among this humiliating farrago our trio played our three tunes. We didn't bother with 'The Man I Love'.

Les had bought himself an ill-fitting, second-hand tuxedo – maybe from the zither shop though he never revealed his sources. It looked as if it had been made to measure for a small horse. Barry and I wore regulation charcoal grey suits with clip-on bow-ties from Woolworth's.

Under the influence of the City Hall concerts we also discussed the possibility of wearing dark glasses but decided against it, on the basis that we needed to see the notes we were playing. Les, who played totally random notes anyway, disagreed but was outvoted two to one. He took the decision badly, like a true democrat.

We got what I've now learned to call mixed reviews. One or two sixth form girls said we looked terrific.

'But what about the music?' we asked our favourite teacher, a robust ex-serviceman who drank at the same pub as we did, but insisted we use different bars during school hours.

'Well,' he said, 'at least you didn't go on as long as that bloody conjuror.'

The headmaster, while grateful for the contribution towards his new dome, was deeply concerned at the use of the grand piano on behalf of Stan Kenton and Pinetop Smith. He instituted a new rule whereby the piano was only to be used for music officially approved, in writing, by our music teacher.

That was the end of the trio. Eventually I sold my guitar to Les, when he went to Leeds University to study psychology.

As I handed the instrument over he said:

'Oh, by the way, I haven't got any money. It'll have to be hire purchase.'

'That's OK,' I said.

As a matter of fact, he still owes me thirty bob but, hell, that's what friends are for. I owe him more that he will ever know, but I'm still trying to figure out whether I should be grateful.

When the Anorak All-Stars Play the Blues

During my teenage, guitar-playing years, I became an anorak. I read the *Melody Maker* and had dreams of seeing my name among the personnel in the top bands of the day. The names of musicians became as important as those of footballers. To this day I can still recite the Sunderland team that won the FA Cup in 1937, when I was two years old, and if I concentrated very hard I could probably recall most of the guys in the Ted Heath band I saw at the City Hall in the 1950s.

This makes me an associate member of the Union of Ultimate Fans, who know who depped on the alternate takes on the unknown bootleg recordings of Charlie Parker with Andy Kirk's Clouds of Joy, to give a random example; and distant cousin to the Yorkshireman who said to Wild Bill Davison: 'You're my fourth favourite trumpet player.' Davison's answer is on the record but not one I'm prepared to set down in print.

These lyrics were written as a tribute to all those fans and also to the musicians who, in some cases anyway, are memorable for the eccentricity of their names rather than for their playing.

Alan Barnes and I are still trying to get this one right: call it a work in progress.

> When the Anorak All-Stars play the blues
> You hear the guys who've paid their dues
> They play the gig, they do the show
> The names that only the anoraks know

Early doors they all get cracking
With Toshiko Akiyoshi and Lew Tabackin
Later on things get unruly
With Cleanhead Vinson and Boots Mussulli
And then we wish upon a star
With Peanuts Hucko and Nappy Lamare

The sun goes down we show them how
With Buddy Featherstonehaugh – like wow!

Trading fours on Giant Steps
Ulysses Livingston, George Van Eps
Vincent Herring and Bobby Few
Do the same on Tea for Two
Playing changes on Midnight Sun
Hannibal Peterson and Teddy Bunn
Putney Dandridge, Dardanelle Hadley,
Want you to know they love you madly
Round about midnight the legends show
Lester, Billie, Earl and Joe
Ella, Louis, Bix and Bill,
Ben and Dizzy, Miles and Gil,
Ornette, Django, Slim and Slam,
Big Sid, Ray and Roy and Sam,
Bubber, Jelly Roll and Duke
Bean and Bud and Sweets and Klook
Big Tea, Sweet Pea, Teddy and Bunk
Big Joe, Big Mo, Eddy and Monk

Comes the dawn and comes the yawn
The stars have gone but the band plays on
The guys who never ever refuse
The chance to play the Anorak Blues

The legendary Clarence Hutchenrider
First with Cherokee then with Ida
J. C. Higginbotham, E. O. Pogson
Play Your Feet's Too Big with clogs on
You don't know the words then why not whistle
With Milton Banana and Noble Sissle?
In the shops soon on an LP cylinder
Starring Tiger Okoshi and Lucky Millinder
Top of the charts in tomorrow's news
The Anorak All Stars play the Blues

(Then a sort of ride-out. . .)
Sumudu Jayatilaka
Sings Charlie Parker
Axel Swingenberger
Plays boogie-woogie mazurka

2.

T'Ain't What You Do

My first encounter with professional musicians was in Newcastle in the 1950s. They were not jazz musicians. They were the members of the pit orchestra of the Palace music-hall, now demolished, in the Haymarket. The theatre, like the music-hall tradition generally, was on its last legs and the same applied to several of the musicians.

By this time I was back on my native Tyneside, actively involved in failing a degree in architecture. I had given up wanting to be Oscar Moore or Django Reinhardt, but within twenty minutes of arriving at the university I decided I didn't want to be Christopher Wren or Le Corbusier either. For a start, architecture was much too hard.

I'd been nudged by the school in the direction of architecture because, by the standards of a small sixth form art class in Hull, I could draw a bit. I still can. I can draw a dog or an elephant and people can spot the difference. In the early nineties I was doing some work with good friend, Lenny Henry and, when sending him notes, would attach a drawing of an elephant for their daughter Billie. On one

occasion I forgot and had a slightly hurt note from Lenny:
'No elephant. Have we upset you?'

But being a good architect requires a range of skills way
beyond being able to draw a bit. You have to be a visionary,
a diplomat and a highly accomplished social animal, capable
of schmoozing your way around the golf clubs, rotarians
and planning committees of your chosen universe, simply
to stay in work. This wasn't for me; I was already looking
for a career you could have hiding under a stone, where you
need only go out after dark.

Fortunately, the university provided a perfect setting,
where young people with delusions could live out their
fantasies. Indeed, I would argue that this is the primary
purpose of any university. It might well be the purpose
of life.

Once a year we had a student rag week, another example
of youthful, self-indulgent humiliation in the name of charity. It was the headmaster's observatory revisited. Its

centrepiece was *Rag Revue*, presented twice nightly at the Palace, an obvious setting for fantasies. Together with my new mate, Jim, I explained to the producer what we wanted to do .

'The act's called the Forty-Four Flying Fletchers,' I said.

'The Forty-Four Flying Fletchers?'

'Yes.'

'What do they do?'

'They're a juggling and acrobatic act. They wear string vests, baggy shorts and false moustaches.'

'And who precisely are these Flying Fletchers?'

'There'll be me and Jim and a medical student called Pete. Mind you, he doesn't know about it yet.'

The producer didn't seem entirely convinced.

'Forgive me for pointing this out,' he said, 'but that's only three.'

'We know that. You have to put a slip in the programme saying unfortunately forty-one of the Flying Fletchers are indisposed. With a pulled muscle.'

'Will you do that?'

'What?'

'Stick ten thousand slips in ten thousand programmes?'

'We thought somebody else could do that. We'll be too busy being Flying Fletchers.'

The producer obviously had no idea of the pressures involved in being writer/performers, carving out new frontiers in comedy. He asked an unforgiveable question.

'And what precisely do they do? The Flying Fletchers?'

There was a pause. It was a loin-girding moment.

'Well, since you ask. . . the high spot is invisible juggling.'

'Invisible juggling?'

'With invisible tennis balls. Obviously. They've got to be invisible because we can't actually juggle. We'll get the drummer to do some drum rolls and cymbal clashes and then when we take our bow we'll have a hundred and twenty-seven real tennis balls drop down on top of us from the flies. It's pretty hysterical, yes?'

The producer said nothing. We took it as a resounding yes. What we were doing was inventing alternative comedy way before the phrase had been invented. Of course, we weren't really. We were recycling Spike Milligan and the Marx Brothers but we did take it very seriously.

We were convinced, for example, that odd numbers were funnier than even numbers – hence a hundred and twenty-seven tennis balls. I still think so and have had serious discussions on the subject with my good friend and occasional teaching colleague on writers' workshops, David Nobbs. He generally responds by saying he doesn't give a damn about odd numbers but knows beyond reasonable doubt that place names with a 'k' sound in them are always funny: thus Scunthorpe, Skegness and Heckmondwike. He says Ken Dodd told him this.

My new mate Jim was a willing accomplice in our escapades. Like me, he was destined to struggle with the official chores of passing examinations, but – and perhaps it isn't entirely a coincidence – ended up as a respected and gifted head of a major school of architecture in Scotland. Then, as now, he had a wonderful sense of the absurd and the surreal. I still remember some of his cartoons of the period. A smiling vicar saying to his dinner table guests: 'That's the trouble with beans.' A man in a hotel room ringing reception complaining: 'Somebody's left a woman in my bed.' A suit of armour with a note pinned to the foot reading: 'Two Pints Please'.

The Forty-Four Flying Fletchers produced my first face-to-face encounter with professional musicians. It happened

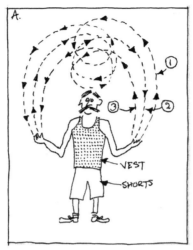

INVISIBLE JUGGLING
A BRIEF INTRODUCTION

at the band call. I explained to the conductor that it would help my invisible juggling if the drummer played along with little drum rolls and an occasional cymbal clash every time I did something extra spectacular.

The orchestra conductor said yes, that was no problem.

'But there's just one thing you have to remember,' he added.

'What's that?'

'You must remember to stand where he can see you.'

'Why's that?' I said.

'Our drummer is as deaf as a post,' said the conductor.

On the night, the act went pretty much according to plan, to the extent that we had a plan. We lost the battle over the slips in the programme. Instead, a willing volunteer from the cast announced:

'Ladies and gentlemen. We proudly present... The

Forty-Four Flying Fletchers. Unfortunately, forty-one of the Flying Fletchers are indisposed with a pulled muscle. Here are the other three.'

We went on, in our string vests, baggy shorts and false moustaches. The high spot of the act was the invisible juggling. The drummer did the kind of spot effects he'd been doing for music-hall acts since the days of Marie Lloyd and Dan Leno – and quite possibly Hadrian, Caedmon and the Venerable Bede. In retrospect, I wonder: what did he think of us? I've got a pretty good idea. Years of working with musicians, especially jazz musicians, have taught me one central truth: if you can make the band laugh, you're on a winner. The converse is also true.

Alarmingly for young self-appointed geniuses hoping to transform the nature of comedy, the audience seemed to enjoy the Flying Fletchers. We would have preferred a bemused silence; but they clapped as we took our curtain call, and laughed as the tennis balls rained down from above. We didn't get the hundred and twenty-seven.

The stage manager, an earnest undergraduate of some proper subject like history or mathematics, had explained: 'We've scoured Newcastle looking for bloody tennis balls. People don't want to give them away. Would you believe, they use them for playing tennis with? You'll have to manage with eighty-five.'

We said it was all right as long as it was an odd number. When he pointed out, pedantically, that the act was called The Forty-Four Flying Fletchers and forty-four was an even number, we put on pained expressions and explained that it wasn't the forty-four that made it funny. The joke was the forty-one who pulled the muscle.

Some people will never understand.

* * *

Jazz was crucial to the student experience. There is a long and honourable history of the music as a central element in schools of art and architecture, as exemplified by Humphrey Lyttelton in London, Sandy Brown in Edinburgh and all points between.

Our version had slightly less of an impact, at the national level anyway. An architecture student called Gordon played trumpet in a student New Orleans revivalist band. They were all, it has to be said, fledgling players. Gordon blew very hard, got very red in the face and not a great deal of interest came out of the other end.

One evening their band gave a recital to the university jazz society. The front line all blew very hard, grew very red in the face and produced enough noise to fill a small room, while we stomped our feet dutifully. Highly sensitive to the jazz tradition, they asked whether anyone in the audience wanted to sit in. Somebody did. He was a young dark-haired man, an English student, and he played the trumpet. His name was Ian Carr and, in the jargon that attends these moments, he blew the roof off.

Gordon was a bit miffed about all this. He muttered darkly: 'He wasn't really improvising. He'd learned all those solos from books and records.'

The curious part of the tale is that I described the evening to Ian Carr, forty years on, and he doesn't remember any of it. I daresay this is the ultimate dilemma of the historian: when the people who were there can't agree on what happened, or even whether they were there at all, what hope is there for historical objectivity? The answer is simple enough. There is no hope at all and the only kind of evidence I believe is strictly anecdotal even if it's mine.

A decade on from the evening in question – whether it happened or not – Ian and his brother Mike were destined to explode on the scene with the EmCee Five, a still unique example of Tyneside-style hard bop.

There were dances every Saturday night in the students' union and the bands generally played in the traditional jazz mode. Itinerant Tyneside musicians who became regulars included a banjo player called Peter Deuchar who was a scion of a major local brewing family and, according to legend, heir to a huge fortune; a mainstream saxophone player called Don Armstrong who led a band called, a tad presumptuously, Armstrong's Hot Five; and a teenage trombone player who looked like Eric Burdon though I've never been able to confirm whether it really was.

The only singer in our midst was Adrian Henri, who was at the art school. Just as my role model at the time was an odd mixture of Spike Milligan, James Thurber and Tennessee Williams, Adrian's was George Melly. He had learned much of George's repertoire, including his version of 'Frankie and Johnny' where he would turn his back on the audience and embrace himself in an unseemly way. It has to be reported that George was better at being George than Adrian was.

After we left university, I didn't see Adrian for twenty-five years, until we were invited on to BBC2's legendary *Late Night Line-Up* – legendary, it has to be said, as much for its drinks cabinet as for the quality of its discussions – when we chatted to Joan Bakewell about weighty matters. I can't remember what they were but I did confirm with Adrian that I hadn't invented my memories of his George Melly performances. He owned up, without shame, but agreed that being a painter and Merseyside poet added up to a more agreeable and apt way of life.

It's only when you look back, as if down the wrong end of a telescope, when everything is distant but in very sharp focus, that obvious truths emerge. It was in my first year that I met a woman destined to be a character in a television film almost half-a-century later.

A fellow-student called Harry suggested we move into a flat. He was a local guy living at home at the time and I was living with my Grandma and Auntie May in Jarrow. I was, in the time-honoured phrase, spoilt rotten. On the other hand, I was limited in my social activities by the tyranny of the last train and the need to be reasonably sober when I arrived home.

Harry's motives were very simple. He wanted a place to take girls to. He was a good and skilful designer, a fine draughtsman but, like me, somewhat irregular in his attendance at lectures. He had a good line in fecklessness and taught me valuable lessons. The first was that the only thing to do with a university grant was to spend it. The second was that having a bank overdraft would never cause the sky to fall. He invented the concept of student debt fifty years before Tony Blair's new model socialists had the idea.

We found a flat along the Elswick Road in the west end of the city, in an area euphemistically said to have 'character'. It has even more character now than it did then and people write letters to the papers about it.

We rented the first floor of a large Victorian house for three pounds a week. The rooms were huge, high and freezing. Our landlady was small, spiky and, during the initial negotiations, unrelentingly nice. She forced cake upon us and told us of the young men – mostly medical students – who had passed through her care and now sent her photographs of their weddings and, with the passing years, of their children.

It all stopped soon after we moved in. Icicles formed,

first on the walls and then on our relationship. Our only source of heat was a coal fire. We had our own coal-shed in the back yard and our landlady arranged for a bag of coal to be delivered to it, on our behalf, as long as we gave her the money in advance. The coal arrived.

We only lit a fire occasionally. We rarely got home before closing time and it was quicker and easier to put on an extra pullover or, in very cold weather, an overcoat and a scarf. In any case, lighting a fire was very difficult, if you hadn't take the precaution of laying in a stock of firewood or fire-lighters. We actually developed and refined our own form of firelighter, using stale Weetabix sprinkled with sugar.

About the second or third time we lit a fire Harry, who had gone down to the back yard to fill the coal bucket, returned with an announcement:

'That bloody woman is stealing our coal.'

According to his analysis, the size of the heap had gone down disproportionately to the number of fires we had lit.

Unrelenting in his pursuit of the truth, Harry later concluded that she was also stealing our tea and sugar.

She didn't help her case by her attitude to our music. By skilful use of our grants and the newly-discovered overdraft facility we had bought a record-player, one of the new-fangled affairs with three speeds and reversible stylus. This left us with sufficient cash-flow for one record each. Mine was the Duke Ellington *Tattooed Bride* album that I later wrote to him about. Harry's was an LPs worth of Wagner's *Lohengrin*.

There is an ancient tradition among architecture students that the days are for sleeping and slobbing, the evenings are for going to the pub, and you do your work after dark, starting around midnight. We were happy to honour the tradition and we naturally laboured over our drawing-boards accompanied by Wagner and The Duke, turn and turn about.

Our landlady was quick to complain.

'You were playing your music again last night.'

'That's because we were working.'

'You had the lights on as well.'

'That's because we were working.'

'My other young men never worked at night.'

'That's because they were medical students and we are architects.'

She wasn't impressed with our explanations. We discussed the situation at length.

'What's her problem?' said Harry.

'It seems to me,' I said, 'that either she doesn't like Duke Ellington or she doesn't like Wagner. Or architects. Or it's purely personal and she doesn't like us.'

'She doesn't like anybody or anything,' said Harry. 'And she's been at our bloody biscuits.'

'Well, at least she likes biscuits.'

We only lasted one term. We packed in a hurry and in my haste I left behind the cord from my dressing-gown. It was nothing fancy: little more than a high-class piece of string. When I called at the house to collect it, she demanded five shillings for its return. I muttered something about not having had time to go to the bank and when she protested I muttered something else about taking advice from a (totally imaginary) law student friend. I gave her sixpence and left with the dressing-gown cord.

But writers always win in the end. Fifty years later I wrote a screenplay that became a BBC TV film called *Doggin' Around*.

It was about Joe Warren, a grizzled American jazz pianist, memorably played by Elliott Gould, gigging around the North of England, accompanied by a minder. Along the way the two characters wind up staying at a stereo-typically ghastly B & B in an unspecified dark corner of Lancashire. The establishment is run by an equally stereotypical landlady, who was brought to wonderfully bizarre life by the totally amazing Liz Smith.

She has draconian rules about times of meals, the lock-ing of the front door and the use of electricity. Any variation from the statute book can only be done by prior arrangement.

'And you can be bricked up with a nun of your choice,' growls Warren, 'but only by prior arrangement.'

He further concludes that she is the estranged wife of Vlad the Impaler and addresses her thereafter as Mrs Vlad, though she doesn't notice. The big shoot-out occurs when they return late from a gig, open up the bar using skills Warren has refined during a brief prison sentence in the States, unlock the piano and have a quiet jam.

She explodes into their midst, complaining about the music at this time of night, and their reckless use of the electricity.

'Because thou art so virtuous, Mrs Vlad, shall there be no more cakes and ale?' says Warren, adding, when she splut-ters further objections: 'That's William Shakespeare, for Christ's sake!'

'There's a time and place for Shakespeare,' she says and throws them out.

It was only when we watched the film on its initial transmission that I realised what I had done. Mrs Vlad was actually our old landlady from the Elswick Road.

And don't make the mistake of thinking she represents a vanished species. We had a similar confrontation with a seaside landlady as recently as the year 2004 A.D.

'I knew it was a mistake to have jazz musicians in my hotel,' she said, when we complained, very gently, about being woken up at nine-thirty in her mistaken belief that we would want breakfast after a late night drinking session with Alan Barnes, Martin Taylor and a group of like-minded souls. Had we wanted breakfast we would have got up. In any case, we could smell the food from our room. But I was thrilled to be classified as a jazz musician and had to be forcibly restrained from spray-painting MRS VLAD LIVES on the walls of her establishment after we checked out.

It was at another meeting of the university jazz club that an alien sound crept into our consciousness, crapped and crept out again. One of the members was giving a lecture on some suitably abstruse aspect of our chosen music, illustrated with records; but he started by playing Bill Haley's 'Rock Around the Clock'.

We all laughed. We thought it was a good joke. Rock was obviously a passing fancy and in time would go. To be sure, the film of the same name had recently opened in Newcastle, and the local burghers had braced themselves for teenage riots and similar manifestations of youthful rebellion. As far as I recall, nothing much happened. There were kids on Tyneside who would happily slash the seats in cinemas if they'd been watching Anna Neagle in *Spring in Park Lane*. In those circumstances one or two of us would happily have joined in.

We added to the turmoil of the debate with a cod news item in one of the various student papers that we were working on at the time. Headlined DANCE HALL RIOT! the story ran:

'There was a serious outbreak of violence following an afternoon tea dance at the Old Assembly Rooms. Gangs of old age pensioners, inflamed by the sensual and pulsating rhythms of the Lancers and the Gay Gordons, went on the rampage through Eldon Square, brandishing their handbags in a threatening manner. Two elderly women are assisting the police in their inquiries. They are believed to be nuns. Though why the police are employing nuns remains a mystery.'

Bill Haley wasn't the only cloud on our cool horizon. We had gone to the Empire, then a number one variety theatre, attracted by the billing of Tony Crombie's Rock and Roll Rockets. We knew Crombie as a jazz drummer. We were not at all impressed by his Rockets. It's possible that he wasn't either. But these were all straws in the wind and we underestimated the strength of the wind and the thickness of the straws.

The fact is we didn't know rock was going to destabilise and, for a while, apparently destroy our jazz world and all who dwelt therein. The evidence, in the mid-fifties, was that the music was healthy and so was its audience. The City Hall in Newcastle was packed out regularly for artists as diverse as Big Bill Broonzy ('Tonight I'm going to sing you some folk songs. Leastways, I guess they're folk songs. I ain't never heard a hoss singing any of them') and the Gerry Mulligan Quartet. The Mulligan concert was punctuated by loud cries from a Geordie fan who kept shouting out: 'What about "Bernie's Tune"?' though in the local vernacular it naturally came out as 'Bornie's Tuen'.

Eventually Mulligan gave way, stepped forward to the microphone and murmured gently: 'I think it's a very nice tune.' And then they played it.

To be sure, Tyneside audiences were never inhibited about joining in, even at the cinema. We went to see an early Sidney Poitier movie called *A Man is Ten Feet Tall,* which, briefly summarised, offered the daring thought that, even in America, a black man could be as brave and dignified as a white man – i.e. ten feet tall. At a key moment in the drama, when the Poitier character was showing signs of weakness, a loud voice from the gallery called out: 'Gan canny, bonny lad. You're back down to five foot six.'

GOOD HEAVENS! - NOT THE DIZZY GILLESPIE?

But the enthusiasm that filled the City Hall was total and uncompromising. We saw our heroes in the flesh: Eddie Condon, Jack Teagarden, Ella Fitzgerald and Oscar Peterson. Bliss was it on those nights to be alive.

We mustn't forget the local heroes. The Chris Barber band invariably played to full houses with their cutting edge brand of revivalism: 'Bobby Shaftoe' always went down a treat. We heard the Dankworth big band with Cleo Laine, and had you told me that one day I would work with both John and Cleo I would have given you directions to the nearest institution for the terminally deluded.

The memories mingle in a kaleidoscope of images and music. The Kirchin Band – largely forgotten these days but for a while one of the wildest outfits around, operating in the Dizzy Gillespie big band tradition – played in the city on the same day that Tottenham Hotspurs had played Newcastle United at St James' Park. A large group of Spurs supporters turned up at the City Hall that night. There's an astonishing thought to look back on: the idea of football supporters seeing a jazz concert as part two of a double-header. There was no need to segregate anyone, either at the match or the concert. Those, indeed, were the days. The Kirchin Band eventually ended up as house band at a ballroom in Hull, where Basil lived until his death in 2005.

I developed an enduring affection for the Mick Mulligan Band (known in the trade, according to our contacts, as 'the band that refuses to improve') and their featured vocalist, George Melly. They seemed destined to play support to many of the visiting Americans, including Broonzy and Eddie Condon. George was also destined to have a walk-on part in my life – a rare example of his being anything else than centre-stage; but more of that anon.

Historically, if not musically, the greatest night of all was the visit of the Louis Armstrong All-Stars. We went with high expectations. We had just discovered the Hot Five and Hot Seven recordings and our heads were full of 'West End Blues' and 'Weatherbird'. What we were presented with on the night was Louis with 'full supporting bill' which included, to our dismay, the one-legged tap dancer, Peg Leg Bates.

Bates was, in truth, a wonderfully talented and courageous man. He would spin on his wooden leg while executing dance steps with the remaining leg. Then he would take his weight on the good leg while using the wooden leg as a drum stick. Throw in a few somersaults and back flips and you get a sense of the act.

But we had gone to hear Louis playing the pure music. We were not impressed by a one-legged tap dancer. We would not have been impressed by a two-legged tap dancer or even a three-legged tap dancer. I shouted out: 'Bring on the dancing girls,' and was shut up by my mates, who didn't want us to be thrown out before we'd even seen Louis himself. After all, we'd paid half-a-crown in old money to get in.

Whether Bates belonged in a jazz concert is neither here nor there. He brought the house down everywhere he played. A few years ago Alan Barnes wrote a cracking instrumental called 'Pops and the Peg Leg' as an act of homage to a remarkable man and, in time, I'll add my supplementary apology by writing some lyrics to go with it, thereby achieving total redemption.

Incidentally, those who would like to know more about one-legged variety acts should read Michael Kilgarriff's wonderful book, *Grace, Beauty and Banjos*.

As for Louis himself, when he walked onstage I shed a tear, though I was naturally careful not to let my mates see. The music that followed was frankly a bit perfunctory, despite the presence in the band of Trummy Young, Billy Kyle and the great Edmond Hall; but knowing what we do now about the almost inhuman touring schedules that Louis endured, it's a miracle we heard any notes at all from the most famous trumpet player in history.

The school of architecture, geographically and spiritually, was next door to the art school which, at the time, was home to such aesthetic luminaries as the pioneering pop artist, Richard Hamilton, and the abstractionist, Victor Pasmore. The art students were a wild and hairy lot and Jim and I found common cause with many of them:

notably a love of the surreal, though I think we would have classified it as Dadaist Revivalism.

Once a year there was the Arts Ball, modelled on the Chelsea Arts Ball which frequently scandalised the more self-righteous newspapers of the day. It was rumoured that Victor Pasmore himself had achieved his limp by breaking his thigh while riding a bicycle down the stairs on one such occasion.

The word went out. The Arts Ball was looking for volunteers to perform cabaret acts. Jim and I were eager to cooperate. We had to explain ourselves to the committee.

'The act's called The Great Prudhoe,' I said.

'I thought Prudhoe was a mining village west of Newcastle,' said a sceptical committee member.

'It is. It's also the name of the act.'

'Who is Prudhoe and what does he do?'

'He's an escapologist. That's to say, he'll be me. I'll be wearing a string vest, baggy shorts and a false moustache.'

It was the same costume I had worn as a member of the Flying Fletchers, an act which continued to have some sort of fame around the campus. Maybe for that reason, the organisers wanted to know more before making any sort of firm commitment.

'What happens next?' asked the sceptic.

'Jim will bind me in chains.'

'And then...?

'I'll be put into a coffin.'

'And then...?'

'Well, nothing. I'll fail to escape and after a bit Jim'll get some volunteers to carry me out. The point about The Great Prudhoe being that he's not a very good escapologist. It's a homage to failure.'

There was a silence, of a sort we were used to when explaining our ideas to people. Jim played the trump card.

'We see it as surrealism with a touch of Dadaist revivalism.'

'Really?'

We could see the committee beginning to waver. I moved in for the kill.

'And don't forget. Jim will be wearing a string vest, baggy shorts and a false moustache as well.'

These days The Great Prudhoe would probably be called a piece of conceptual art. However you define it, we got the gig. On the night, it went exactly according to plan, to the extent that we had a plan. The setting was the Oxford Galleries, the major dance-hall in Newcastle where, during the war, the great saxophonist Kathleen Stobart had served her apprenticeship. At the appointed hour, a space was cleared on the dance-floor. Jim and I walked on in our string vests, baggy shorts and false moustaches. I was bound in chains and placed in the coffin from which, Jim announced, The Great Prudhoe would escape. I did not escape. Nothing happened at all. The initial reaction from the audience was mute incomprehension. Even from inside the coffin I could sense the apathy. That seemed about right. It proved we were ahead of our time.

Soon the apathy gave way to boredom, then, since most of those present were under the influence of Newcastle Brown Ale, sullen hostility took over. The coffin was hoisted on to the shoulders of half-a-dozen volunteers we had prepared earlier. The Great Prudhoe, under-achieving escapologist, was carried from the dance-floor while a student band played a barely recognisable version of 'The Dead March'.

Obviously, because I was inside the coffin, I was unable

to appreciate the quality of the moment but Jim later assured me the atmosphere was one of majestic anti-climax. In our terms, that made it a triumph.

For me, the true excitement was still to come. We ended up backstage in the bandroom and when I was released the first person I saw was George Melly. He was waiting to go on with the Mick Mulligan Band, the night's star attraction. That was key to the spirit of the times; you couldn't have an Arts Ball without a traditional jazz band.

I stood beside the coffin in my string vest, baggy shorts and false moustache, the chains lying at my feet. George didn't bat an eyelid. Jazz musicians are, of course, legendary for their ability to be unimpressed by anything. Aside from that, George was already one of the nation's leading experts on surrealism. Indeed, you could argue that his entire life and career have been a wondrous surrealist adventure. From his point of view, in the surrealist stakes, The Great Prudhoe didn't even come under orders.

There's a tag to the tale. Forty years on, I did a radio programme with George – a show described by my wife as 'two old farts rambling on about jazz', which is about right. Chatting to George, I reminded him of our first meeting: backstage at the Oxford Galleries when I was being let out of the coffin and the chains and he was preparing to go on with Mick's band.

'Do you remember?' I said.

'No,' said George.

I was quite relieved to hear it; though what I should have said was that, for me, it was an event of great historical significance. It was the first time I had met a fully-fledged professional jazz musician. Life would never be the same again, but perhaps it never was.

Everyone's Got to Be Somewhere (for Spike Milligan)

During our student years, *The Goon Show* was our gospel and Spike Milligan was God. This was despite the fact that we couldn't hear it properly. It was an innocent era, totally free of transistor radios, I-pods, ghetto blasters. If you wanted ambient sound you had to make your own.

Once a week we made our pilgrimage to the common room in the students' union where there was a radio mounted high on the wall. Unfortunately the reception wasn't very good and the volume was low. What we heard was virtually incoherent; but that didn't worry us. It was an act of worship at the shrine. We laughed when the studio audience laughed and nodded knowingly to each other. We had joined an exclusive club and we were life members.

These lyrics were inspired by an old *Goon Show* gag that ran something like: 'What are you doing there, Eccles?' Eccles replies: 'Everybody's got to be somewhere.'

> There was an old woman who lived in a shoe
> There was a young tiger who lived in a zoo
> And a green-eyed yellow idol in Katmandu
> Well – everyone's got to be somewhere
> Shoe – zoo – Katmandu
> Everyone's got to be somewhere
>
> There's a dairymaid called Daisy on the Isle of Mull
> There's a groupy name of Maisy hanging loose in Hull
> And a geezer going crazy out in Istanbul
> Well – everyone's got to be somewhere
> Mull – Hull – Istanbul
> Everyone's got to be somewhere

Everybody's got to be somewhere
That's the gospel according to Spike
So groove – don't move – just stand right there
And stay well away from that bike

There's a DNA component that lives in cells
There's a guy called Quasimodo who lives in bells
There's a very angry colonel in Tunbridge Wells
See? – everyone's got to be somewhere
Cells – bells – Tunbridge Wells
Everyone's got to be somewhere

There's a guy called Jacky Horner who lives on pie
There's an aging sixties hippy from the Isle of Skye
Now he's permanently way on high in Hay-on-Wye
Like – everyone's got to be somewhere
Pie – Skye – Hay-on-Wye
Everyone's got to be somewhere

Somewhere is better than nowhere
Even if it isn't so hot
Look around and you'll see somewhere
But if you're nowhere – face it – you are not

There's a scat cat singer who inhabits the blues
There's an alcoholic drummer who inhabits the booze
While their jazz promoter's on the run in Santa Cruz
Yeah! – everyone's got to be somewhere
Blues – booze – Santa Cruz
Everyone's got to be somewhere

Shoe – zoo – Katmandu
Everyone's got to be somewhere

Mull – Hull – Istanbul
Everyone's got to be somewhere
Cells – bells – Tunbridge Wells
Everyone's got to be somewhere
Pie – high – isle of Skye
Everyone's got to be somewhere
Blues – booze – Santa Cruz
Everyone's got to be somewhere
Not to mention. . .
Brent – Kent – Stoke-on-Trent
Poole – Goole – Hartlepool
Leek – Speke – up shit creek
Everyone's got to be – guess where?

3.

Hot Time in the Old Town

Journalists in recent times have fallen in love with the phrase 'defining moments' – though all too often, as time passes, nobody can remember what it was the moment was supposed to define. You need to be years, possibly decades, removed from them to be sure that they defined anything that matters a damn.

From a safe distance I can now write, with total certainty, that I had a clutch of these moments as the 1950s lurched into sixties. They probably didn't matter much to anyone else but they were crucial to me.

The first was in 1957 when Professor Edwards, head of the school of architecture, suggested it would be better for him, me and the built environment, if we went our separate ways. This was at the end of the fourth year of the five year course. Since I had failed all but one of the end-of-year examinations he had reason and logic on his side. My mate Jim was thrown out at the same time, for much the same official reasons, though we decided it was because he hadn't enjoyed The Forty-Four Flying Fletchers.

In fairness, the Prof was a genial man underneath his rather gruff North Wales exterior. He actually liked us, for reasons difficult to fathom, and celebrated our departure by organising an official pub crawl around Northumberland, with members of staff trawled in as designated volunteer drivers for the night.

I took the coward's way out: I returned to Hull and got a proper job, in an architect's office. It was a small private practice run by an amiable man called Brian and staffed by a group of cheerful anarchists, none of whom wanted to be remembered by posterity for their services to hard labour. We worked, when all the alternative possibilities had been explored and rejected, in a dusty, Dickensian attic in Scale Lane, in the heart of Hull's mediaeval Old Town.

It was another defining moment: it defined that a proper job wasn't for me. You had to be there at nine o'clock

YOU'VE BUILT IT UPSIDE DOWN
(OLD ARCHITECTURAL JOKE)

every morning and you were expected to stay there until five. To be sure, the company was congenial. There was Eric, our quantity surveyor, and a reliable purveyor of old jokes, thus:

'I say, I say, I say, what is the difference between a warhorse and a carthorse?'

'I don't know, Eric. What is the difference?'

'A warhorse darts into the fray.'

There was Bernard, our office boy, who fetched our lunchtime cheese-and-pickle sandwiches from Charlie Foster's shop along the lane, housed in the oldest building in the area. Bernard was a relentless singer of current pop songs. The Jerry Lee Lewis hit, 'Great Balls of Fire,' was a special favourite and would often provoke the exchange:

'Bernard!'

'What?'

'Shut up!'

'I think I'll shut up.'

It also occurs to me, dredging in this memory bank, that there is a character in *Doggin' Around*, a dedicated jazz anorak, played by Alun Armstrong. I called him Charlie Foster, and it was probably a subconscious homage to a celebrated maker of cheese-and-pickle sandwiches.

There was George, an immaculate draughtsman of the old school, who spent at least half his office hours running his own private practice, and whose son played in a local skiffle group. The latter popped into the office one day for morning coffee and announced that he'd got a new girlfriend.

'We go dancing,' he said.

'Ballroom?' said Eric.

'Can't complain.'

There was a deal of overlap between architecture and jazz, in Hull, as everywhere else. Eddie Anderson (washboard, guitar, drums) worked across the lane for an architect called Roper-Spencer who underlined his fidelity to the hyphen by wearing plus-fours or 'shit-stoppers' as Eric called them. Keith Smith (clarinet) and Glen Gibb (trombone) worked in the City Architect's department of the Council and were part of a gang who would meet for lunch every Friday in Ye Olde White Harte where once upon a time the local republicans had plotted against King Charles, refusing him entrance to the city when he was on the run. We didn't plot against the crown. We talked aesthetics and jazz, with an occasional game of snooker thrown in. It was the heyday of the long lunch and I'd sometimes have a little nap on my drawing-board of a Friday afternoon.

Though it was a convivial way of life, in good company, I was busy digging my escape tunnel. Still convinced I was the next James Thurber, I churned out pieces, notably for *Punch* and braced myself for their rejection. They never let me down until, in 1958, another defining moment came along. I sold something. I can still remember the letter from the editor, Bernard Hollowood.

'Thank you for sending "The Artificial Respiration Controversy", which I like very much and hope to use in the near future.'

The piece appeared and I was paid fifteen guineas, at a time when I was on ten pounds a week. I spent twenty of the guineas on a record-player. That seemed a proper economic policy for a professional writer – one that Thurber himself would have approved of.

It also solved a major domestic problem. I had returned from university with a tiny clutch of records: among them the Ellington LP and a ten inch LP of Louis Armstrong's *New York Town Hall Concert*. The sleeve of this one was later seen in *The Beiderbecke Tapes*. In the opening episode Trevor Chaplin has moved in with Jill Swinburne and she looks on in horror as he unpacks his record collection.

'I'd forgotten this one,' he says. 'It's a ten inch LP. They don't make these any more. I think it cost ten shillings. Do you remember shillings?'

Lesson one for a writer: never let anything go to waste.

I quit the office at the end of the 1950s. On January lst 1960, I became self-employed and have stayed that way ever since. In the words of the fine Tyneside playwright, Tom Hadaway: 'It is the proper condition of mankind.' I started calling myself a writer though the supporting evidence was slender. Occasional pieces for the *Architects' Journal* at five guineas a time; book reviews for the *Yorkshire Post* at two guineas a time, though they let you keep the book; six lousy plays that nobody wanted and a further garland of rejection slips from *Punch*.

But at least I could play my records again and had Duke Ellington's Famous Orchestra and the Louis Armstrong All-Stars to sing me to my rest.

One of my best friends at school was Tom Courtenay and we have stayed pals ever since. He was younger than I was. He still is. Consequently he was able to avoid being dragged into ludicrous sketches for sixth form concerts, but in adolescence we occasionally shared our secret dreams – his of becoming an actor, mine of becoming a writer. I revealed this when I appeared on his *This Is Your Life*, adding:

'I don't think we believed it would ever happen but now it has, all I can say is, it couldn't have happened to two nicer fellers.'

Tom, along with Albert Finney, became one of the iconic figures of the Swinging Sixties. I didn't. I was a young married man, with three kids – born 1962, 1964 and 1966 – and most of the time sat at my desk working, with occasional brief forays to Leeds, Manchester and London as people started to take an interest in my plays. As far as I was concerned, the Swinging Sixties were a loud noise coming from the next street, a party I hadn't been invited to. It was made worse because the music coming from the party wasn't even jazz.

I did my best. My first radio play was broadcast in 1961. It was an elephantine political satire called *The Smokeless Zone* which had, as its opening and closing music, the Kid Ory recording of 'Maryland My Maryland'. Old comrades will know it is the same tune as 'The Red Flag'.

It seemed obvious that the play must be preserved for posterity. Vanity of vanities, all is vanity. I bought a tape recorder from Fanthorpe's, a second-hand shop in the Old Town arcade and duly recorded the play by placing the microphone on its little plastic stand in front of the radio. The result was probably the lowest-fi since the early wax cylinders. Years later I decided to listen to it again. Five minutes in I gave up. It's bad enough when a young writer thinks he's funny but even worse when he's out to change the world and knows exactly how to do it. I decided Kid Ory was the only bit of the play worth listening to and binned the tape. With a bit of luck the BBC will have done the same.

But the 1960s were a good time for young writers. Bliss was it in that decade to be alive, but to be an emerging playwright was very heaven. Television drama was expanding, there weren't enough refugees from radio and the film business to fill all those hours, and most theatre writers were a bit sniffy about television. Some of them still are. So we were in demand. It's a good thing to be and much better than the alternative.

It was also an age of innocence. Making television plays was a cottage industry and the general reaction to any idea was: let's try it. I starting work with Vivian Daniels, who was head of drama for the BBC in the North Region. He was producer, director and script editor and his official function was to supply eight plays a year to the network. He did all this without reference to London.

MAN - THAT'S REALLY WAY OUT
(MY 1960'S JOKE)

The plays were produced in the Dickenson Road studio in Manchester. This was an old church hall which, in the thirties and forties, had been the headquarters of Mancunian Films. Here they had made immensely popular, low-budget comedies starring legends like Sandy Powell, George Formby and Frank Randle.

The films had great innocence and in many ways we continued that tradition. It worked like this. In 1963 I wrote a play for Vivian called *A Smashing Day*. It was the second time we'd worked together and I now had the courage to have opinions on what we were doing and even express some of them out loud.

'I didn't like the captions on the last play,' I said.

'Are you beating me over my head with your architectural training?'

'Well, yes, a bit. We did Roman lettering in first year. And some of the modern type faces in second year. Obviously you can't design a decent building if you can't do proper lettering.'

Vivian gave me a look.

'In that case you'd better make your own captions. Anything else?'

'Yes. I've just bought an EP of Mose Allison's *Back Country Suite*. I thought it might work quite well as the opening music.'

'Bring it with you to the studio. Along with the caption cards. Anything else? The inner meaning of the play? The characters and their relationships?'

'Not really.'

I've never been any good at all that inner meaning stuff. That's for the audience to decide.

'Any thoughts on casting?' said Vivian.

'Yes. When I go to London I generally stay with Tom Courtenay in Highbury and his flat-mate's called John Thaw. He comes from Manchester. Moss Side I think. He's a really good lad.'

'Have you seen him act?'

'No, but I've been to the pub with him. And they've got this terrific Cannonball Adderley LP...'

'John Thaw.'

Vivian wrote the name down.

On the day everything went pretty well according to plan, to the extent that there was a plan. I turned up in Dickenson Road with my caption cards and my Mose Allison EP, and we recorded the play, starring John Thaw with Alfred Lynch, June Barry and Angela Douglas. When it was shown, I got my first rave notice. One critic said: 'It had the voice of *Coronation Street* but the spirit of Chekhov.'

I rushed off to the Central Library in Hull, a vital ingredient in my life for many years, planted my tickets on the desk and said: 'Give me everything in this building by or about Anton Chekhov.'

The play was also seen by Peter Cheeseman, who ran the Victoria Theatre in Stoke-on-Trent. We'd done a couple of shows together and he was very keen to do a stage version of *A Smashing Day.*

'But,' he said when we met to discuss it, 'let's do it as a play with music.'

Plays with music were very much in vogue, thanks mainly to the pioneering work of the great renegade, Joan Littlewood, at the Theatre Royal, Stratford East. It's generally forgotten that her original production of Shelagh Delaney's *A Taste of Honey* was punctuated by music from a live, onstage jazz group and Brendan Behan, famously, couldn't get through a play or a day in his life, without songs. There was nothing new in any of this. Three hundred and fifty years earlier, William Shakespeare had used songs as a key ingredient in the drama. I've always argued that the final part of *Twelfth Night* should be sub-titled, *Feste Sings the Blues*.

I agreed with Peter that songs would be a good idea. The play was on the short side in any case and music would pad it out a bit.

'Who can we get to write the music?' I said.

'I thought we'd ask the Beatles,' said Peter.

'But they're all multi-millionaires. What will you use for money?'

The theatre, naturally, was broke. The heating only worked spasmodically and on winter nights you could not only hear the dialogue, you could see it, in vapour form, floating from the actors' mouths across the stage.

Peter wasn't worried about penury.

'We'll offer them the same deal we did with the Highwaymen.'

'The Highwaymen?'

'They're a local group. They did the music for a production last year.'

'What was their deal?'

'Complimentary tickets for life.'

Peter wrote to Brian Epstein, enclosing a copy of the script, and asking whether John and Paul might like to write some songs for us. I don't know whether he explained the small print of the deal. Brian totally ignored the request but fell in love with the play.

It went into production with music written by our two young assistant stage managers, Ben Kingsley and Robert Powell. They weren't yet good enough to be acting in plays, but they could sing and play guitars. My guess is they both probably wanted to be Bob Dylan but I never thought to ask them at the time. It was their music that Brian Epstein heard when he came up to Stoke to see the play.

His visit caused much excitement. He flew up in a private plane landing – according to urban myth – at an old

RAF airfield specially reopened for his visit. From there he travelled to the theatre in a chauffeur-driven limo.

He took us all for a drink in the local pub after the show and later put on the play at London's Arts Theatre. John Lennon, Ringo Starr and Cilla Black came to the first night. At the party afterwards I asked John whether he had liked our songs.

'Not very much.'

I didn't bother to point out that, had he written the songs for us, not only would he have liked them, he would have had complimentary tickets for life at the Victoria Theatre, Stoke-on-Trent.

A Smashing Day was my first West End flop. The critics were lukewarm and very few people saw it. It was Brian's second production in the theatre, and the last before he died. The first was James Baldwin's *The Amen Corner* which, despite good notices, had failed to fill the Shaftesbury Theatre. I figured if you were going to flop, you might as well do it in good company.

The experience in Stoke had a more lasting effect. Driving back from the Potteries one day, the car skidded off the road and ended up in collision with a dry-stone wall in Derbyshire. I was wearing a new-fangled safety belt and was totally unhurt. The car radio was on and Dusty Springfield was singing 'In the Middle of Nowhere'.

I got out of the car and stood, helpless and alone, as men are wont to do at times of crisis. After a while a farmer appeared from across a field. He greeted me with a kind of long-suffering courtesy. It emerged that this kind of thing happened two or three times a week on this stretch of road. He took me back to the house where his wife gave me tea and offered me lunch, which I declined.

I wasn't feeling very hungry. They rang for help, which duly arrived.

The whole experience left me with a thought. If we had a producing theatre in Hull, I could put on my plays without the perils of a long drive. The city I lived in was not without its hazards but was totally free of country roads and dry stone walls.

I discovered a group of like-minded people, all equally concerned that a city with a population of a quarter of a million didn't have a theatre capable of generating its own drama. We did the only thing possible in a democracy. We formed a committee.

A lovely comedian, the late Tom Mennard, said to us: 'I started a theatre once, and I've got a letter from the bank manager to prove it.'

We should have listened; but we never do. The edited highlights of how we launched our theatre are very simple and straightforward. Between 1965 and 1970 we raised the money and, courtesy of a friendly vicar, found a building – the disused St Stephen's church hall in Spring Street, Hull, in a backwater behind the bus station and handy for the morgue.

We opened the Hull Arts Centre – 'a workshop and show window for all the Arts' – in 1970 and were almost immediately broke. Pretty soon we were on first name terms with the bailiff, a local auctioneer called Gilbert Baitson. In my architect days I had designed a conservatory for him. He'd wander into the lobby and we'd say: 'Good morning, Gilbert, what have you come to take away today? A cup of coffee before you go? We'll give you a hand with the carrying.'

Our penury had a dramatic effect on some of the shows. During a children's play, a scene in the Sahara desert gained considerable impact by the snow falling on to the stage through a hole in the roof.

On the positive side, we developed a unique relationship with the local community, at a time when there still was a local community. In an early production of D. H. Lawrence's *The Daughter-in-Law* we needed a practical – i.e. edible – Yorkshire pudding. Every night for three weeks the landlady of the local pub, the Good Fellowship, made us a perfect Yorkshire pudding. I have never seen such drooling in an audience.

Mina, who lived nearby, in the brief period when there were still houses nearby, became our resident cleaner. One day she arrived to find there had been a break-in overnight. They must have been the most deluded burglars in the history of petty crime. They found nothing of value but left a great deal of mess, which Mina cleared up comprehensively before the forensics people arrived from the police station.

'Well,' she said, 'I couldn't let the police see the place in such a mess.'

We took advice on security from a retired safe-blower – a friend of mine called Dick, whom I met while prison-visiting at Hedon Road Gaol. He looked at our safe (which we might well have bought on the cheap at one of Gilbert's auctions) and once he'd stopped laughing at it, his advice was: 'Dump the safe and find a good hiding place.'

Our response was: 'We would, if we had anything to hide.'

The astonishing fact is that thirty-five years on, the place is still in business, now called the Hull Truck Theatre – the latest in various name changes – marooned in one of those bleak deserts that precede redevelopment. Even the bus station is being demolished to make way for a better bus station and the theatre, including the fragmentary remains of the old church hall, will go the same way. A brand-new, multi-million pound, purpose-built theatre will take its place.

Leisure and the arts, once seen as the obsessions of a lunatic fringe – of which we were founder-members – are now the beating heart of the regeneration agenda in the old industrial communities.

As the great Mr Vonnegut says: so it goes.

Needless to say, I did all I could to integrate music in general and jazz in particular, into our activities. Our opening show – a knockabout musical about the city called *Don't Build a Bridge, Drain the River!* – included songs by Mike Waterson, of the legendary Waterson family who, at that time, lived only ten minutes' walk away.

But prior to the opening of the Centre, we promoted a whole series of events designed to draw attention to the mischief we were planning. Some of them even made money. On the whole we regarded it as a triumph if we broke even on our fund-raisers.

Ironically, one of our best earners was our poetry competition. The method is very simple and apparently standard practice in poetic circles. You charge a modest entry fee. I think ours was a pound, though it might have been ten bob. A fine local poet called George Kendrick, who was on one of our committees, agreed to do the initial scan, after which Philip Larkin would select the winner from the top twenty or so.

I remember George saying: 'It was all right when the poems arrived in bundles. I could just about handle it when the postman arrived with my own sack. It was when

I got my own post office van I realised this thing was out of control.'

Memory says we raised about five hundred quid on the poetry competition but I'm ashamed to say that same memory can't remember who won it.

Meanwhile, in the great big world outside of Hull – in Harrogate to be precise – I had written a Festival play, along with my musical sidekick, Alex Glasgow. In the company was Bari Johnson, a highly-gifted Jamaican-born actor, singer and dancer.

One night a woman in the Harrogate audience asked me: 'Where did you find your wonderful black man?'

'Nottingham,' I said.

Late night at the Festival Club, Bari performed a one-man show called *Ex Africa*, a history of the black experience from the days of slavery to the present day. It seemed to me just the thing we should be doing in Hull and I asked Bari about it.

'Do you want the cheap version or the more expensive version?' he asked.

'What's the difference?'

'The cheap version is me with a tape recorder. The expensive version is me with the Joe Harriott Quartet.'

Joe Harriott!

It was an easy decision and we presented *Ex Africa* on the university campus in the summer of 1968, to raise the local consciousness and make a few bob into the bargain. I think we broke even in both areas.

The audience reaction to the show was, in some ways, characteristic of Hull in that period: it ranged from the ecstatic to the churlish. The social historians didn't like the music and the jazz fans moaned because there wasn't enough of it. A local architect complained that he had never liked crooners, a word I hadn't heard in conversation since the war. And the honorary secretary of a writers' circle wrote to say they weren't coming because seven-and-six seemed 'a bit steep'. Not that any of this still rankles, you understand.

My most vivid memory has nothing to do with the show. It was Joe's arrival in the hall for the sound check. He strolled down the aisle with that elegant, relaxed Jamaican walk. He wore a smart suit and was one of the most handsome men I ever met.

He overnighted with us and this marked the beginning of a relationship that continued to his death in 1973. I hesitate to call it a friendship – perhaps kinship would be a more accurate word. That five-year period saw a catastrophic decline in his career and his health. The man who walked into the hall in the summer of 1968 was cool and confident, the first British-based jazz musician to be hailed in the USA as an artist of genuine world stature. The last time I saw him he was mortally ill and in the depths of despair. As I've said elsewhere: I've known a few tortured artists in my time and Joe was right up there with the best of them.

The causes are not hard to define. His music, always ahead of its time, had no chance in an arena suddenly dominated by the Beatles and all the tribes thereof. Even the trad boom got lost in the rush, not that we shed too many tears about that.

In Hull, as elsewhere, people rallied to the cause, though there were never enough of them. Joe had a list of contacts, compiled over the years of touring, and he would call up: 'Alan? Joe Harriott. I'm coming on the road next month. Halifax and maybe Nottingham. Can you fix me a gig in Hull?'

I called in all the favours I could and gigs for the alto

saxophonist ranged from the memorable to the humiliating, by way of the controversial. The usual arrangement was that Joe would play with a local rhythm section, the best of them led by a piano player called Max Boylett, a student who had run into trouble with the academic authorities because of the length of his hair. How long ago it all seems.

Explaining the controversy involves a brief spasm of social and technological history. There was, and indeed still is, a sturdy history of public ownership in Hull, some of which could easily be mistaken for socialism. For a hundred years the city owned its own telephone services, operating in tandem with the national service run by the GPO. The council then did a deal with a local company called Rediffusion. Years before Margaret Thatcher decided cabling the country was the solution to all our problems and then got it wrong, Hull was transmitting radio and television signals to its housing estates down wires instead of through the air. Sound and pictures were guaranteed free from interference, no small thing in those far-off days when even a neighbourhood motor-bike or hoover could ruin your evening's viewing.

We also had the most popular and enterprising local radio station in the land. BBC Radio Humberside had in its ranks an adventurous – some might say reckless – young producer called Jim Hawkins, who went on to have a fine career as a playwright.

For a while Jim produced a live radio show from our theatre. It was a cheerful ragbag of chat, interviews, local folk plugging their wares and music. Every week, Antony Minghella, then a student in the university drama department, would write and sing a song, accompanying himself on the piano. He was so talented it was scary. It still is.

After one of the radio shows I spoke to Jim.

'Joe Harriott wants to do a gig in Hull. Any chance of recording it? Then we could give him a broadcast fee. Double his earnings for the night.'

'We can do better than that. We'll broadcast it live.'

And so it came to pass – a live transmission from Spring Street starring Joe Harriott with the Steve Marshall Jazz Vehicle, a local rehearsal band, though on this occasion rehearsals played no part in the proceedings. Jim Hawkins, who was presenter as well as producer, had to busk at the microphone between numbers while Joe and the guys agreed what they would play next. It was all very like jazz.

The cause of a resulting controversy was very simple. On the Rediffusion network, BBC Radio Humberside shared a channel with Radio 2. Usually, Radio Humberside only broadcast during the evening on special occasions, like a jazz concert starring Joe Harriott. What we didn't know was that our show coincided with a long-awaited British heavyweight title fight between Henry Cooper and Joe Bugner. The result was that all over Hull sturdy sons of toil, numbering thousands, switched on their radios to hear the big fight and instead heard Joe Harriott playing 'Perdido'.

They were not best pleased. The resulting fuss didn't quite end up with questions in the House but Jim didn't make any more rash commitments without checking carefully in the diary first; meanwhile he had done his duty to a great artist, as befits a producer working for a public service broadcaster.

The saddest gig was the last I was responsible for. Joe, who I later discovered was more or less homeless, was passing through and asked if I could organise for him to play.

'The money doesn't matter. I just need to blow. Is there any place I can play? Just a little bossa nova, I won't do anything to scare anybody.'

I phoned a guy called Frank Brown who ran the Westfield Club in Cottingham, in the leafy suburbs of the city. By our standards, it was top of the range. In the heyday of the Northern club circuit, the Shirley Basseys of the world would appear at regular intervals, playing to packed houses. But the Brown family also had a taste for jazz and both Oscar Peterson and Stephane Grappelli had appeared there.

'Frank. Can you do me a favour? Joe Harriott's in town and needs a blow. Can I bring him down?'

'Why not? There's no cabaret tonight so he could do a spot.'

Joe played a set with the house band, a trio of musicians who, to their surprise and delight, found themselves backing a legend. The place was probably half-full. The punters had come to eat, drink and maybe dance a little, though there was little outward sign of making merry.

Joe played sweet music: a couple of bossa novas, as promised, plus a few standards. He played, as always, like a fallen angel. And he was totally ignored. The only people who applauded were the band and a small group of us standing at the bar. Musically speaking, it was one of the bleakest evenings of my life.

Joe's visits invariably had sequels. They generally went like this. The phone would ring and there would be some local friend or acquaintance on the line.

'Alan, you're a friend of Joe Harriott's. . .'

'Yes.'

'Well, the last time he was here, I lent him twenty pounds.'

'No, you didn't.'

'Yes, I did. I was in the theatre bar after the show and he explained he had to be in Southampton the next day and he hadn't had time to go to the bank. So I lent him twenty pounds.'

'Sorry. You didn't lend him twenty pounds. You *gave* him twenty pounds. You have become a patron of the arts and I thank you on his behalf.'

But there is a rough justice in these matters and it's good that a younger generation of jazz warriors has discovered Joe's music, thanks in part to the efforts of people like his contemporaries, bassist Coleridge Goode and pianist Michael Garrick. And Alan Robertson's biography *Joe Harriott – Fire in His Soul* is a loving testimony to an extraordinary career.

My personal memories are dominated by staying up late into the night, while he drank large quantities of whisky and talked. He told wonderful stories, in that lovely, lilting Caribbean accent. The one that lingers to this day concerned Dizzy Gillespie and the first time Joe played a concert with him.

'We played a couple of numbers and I thought, well, man, he's OK, but really he's just going through the motions. And then, Dizzy took off and all of a sudden he was right up there in the rafters and, man, we were just swallows on the water.'

Joe died of neglect – his own and other people's – on January 2nd 1973, aged 44. I only learned about it from a brief death announcement in the Hull *Daily Mail*, placed there by a girl-friend he had in the area.

Later I wrote a stage play called *Swallows on the Water*. It wasn't about jazz or about Joe but it was about people who aim for the rafters and the price they sometimes pay.

Swallows on the Water (for Joe Harriott)

Over thirty years after his death, Joe's words continued to haunt me. When I started writing songs with Alan Barnes, he and his music demanded tribute and celebration. The words came easily.

Joe blew high
For the swallows on the water
Joe flew high
For the swallows on the water

Playing music only he could hear
Playing music from another sphere
Going places others couldn't go
Going places others didn't know

Joe he came
From an island on the water
Seeking fame
In an island on the water

The island of his dreams it let him down
Dumped him on the dark side of the town
Left him to the mercy of the rain
Left him to the mercy of his pain

Joe he sighed
For the swallows on the water
Joe he died
And the swallows on the water
Cried

4.

Groovin' High

If Joe Harriott was the first jazz musician I came to know personally, the first one I worked with was Tubby Hayes. I can have no complaints about the quality of the company I kept.

The saga began with a film producer called Ken Harper. Ken was a formative influence on my film career. He was a producer of the old school who believed in big cigars, expense accounts, long business lunches at the Ivy and Chez Solange (where I learned to speak menu French) and a philosophy of film-making built outwards from the refrigerated drinks cabinet in his office. He was a tough commercial animal with an appealing line in showbiz cynicism.

'If you're going to get a divorce, make sure you do it when you've just had a bad year.' And, when Kay Walsh asked about her close-ups on the set of *The Virgin and the Gypsy*, he murmured to me: 'Just because she was once married to David Lean, you'd think she'd directed fucking *Zhivago*.'

It was all heady stuff for a kid from the sticks.

Ken was the first producer to trust me to write a screen-play for a movie, the aforementioned *Virgin and the Gypsy*, from D. H. Lawrence's novella. Since he also gave Ken Russell his break in features, he deserves recognition for his courage or recklessness, depending on your point of view.

He had also, in the early sixties, launched Cliff Richard's film career. About this, as about everything, he had a fund of good yarns which he loved to share over the second bottle.

'I was passing through New York while we were casting *Summer Holiday* and had a call from an agent. Had I cast the girl yet? Yes, I'd cast the girl. Why? Turns out he's got a girl. She can act, she can dance, she can sing like an angel. Sorry, I told him, we've already cast Una Stubbs. What's the name of your girl? Barbra Streisand.'

One evening in 1968, Ken took me out for my first out-rageously expensive dinner. There were four of us: Ken and his wife, the director Christopher Miles, and me. We ate at the Carlton Grill which was next door to Ken's apartment. He had an account there and called it his local.

I was in the middle of my most radical socialist phase. Ken knew of my politics and regarded them with a kind of amused contempt. He calculated (correctly) that Marxism was unlikely to catch on in time to damage his expense ac-count.

Nevertheless, up in the North, loyal comrades were col-lecting Ordnance Survey maps of their towns and cities and circling in red the most suitable lamp-posts for hanging the capitalist hyenas. All this being so, I wasn't ideal material for most favoured status at the Carlton Grill.

It didn't help when, at the end of the meal, I glimpsed the bill. Including wine, it was almost ten pounds. I was outraged though I covered up well and said: 'Thank you, Ken, that was a smashing meal.'

The political angst was compounded because the day before I had been to my Auntie May's funeral in Jarrow. May was my mother's elder sister, a tiny woman who never weighed much over five stones, suffered from ill health much of a hard-working life, yet battled through into her seventies. After the funeral, I'd taken the next train from Newcastle to London, to meet Ken and Christopher, to talk about our movie.

Most of May's working life was spent as a wages clerk at Swan Hunter's shipyard in Hebburn, one stop along the River Tyne from Jarrow. The equation that smacked me between the eyes as I stumbled from the Carlton Grill to my hotel was this: the cost of our meal at the Carlton was more than May had ever earned in a week.

I responded like a dramatist should, confronted with life's grotesque injustices: I wrote a play.

The play was called *Rest in Peace, Uncle Fred*.

I observed my standard procedure when writing from personal experience and not wanting to be caught out: I changed everybody's sex and changed the geography as well to be on the safe side.

In the play I became an actress, played by Susan Jameson, being wined and dined by a producer. The previous day, she has been to her Uncle Fred's funeral in Halifax. We cross-cut between the two events – the dinner and the funeral.

I took two enormous liberties by having them eat their meal at a sophisticated West End joint where a small band was playing cool jazz. The music was there to bind the two story strands together: bop as cinematic sellotape. My initial idea was that we should ask Joe Harriott to write and play the music but my director, Michael Hayes (no relation – I checked) was very keen to use Tubbs, because he had worked with him before. I was very happy to go along with this. I was always keen to add another legend to my collection.

The first enormous liberty was that Tubbs probably never played anywhere that served expensive food, a truth that the late Ronnie Scott would have enthusiastically confirmed.

HOW REVOLUTIONS BEGIN
(THE SPIRIT OF 1968)

'Try the food,' Ronnie used to say. 'The chef's rash has nearly cleared up.'

The second enormous liberty – worse than that, unforgiveable – was that my characters talked while the band was playing, which made them unworthy of being in one of my plays in the first place. I filed both liberties under: dramatic licence during my formative period.

The play was transmitted on BBC television in February 1970. Well after midnight the telephone rang. There were no answering machines in those days and telephones had bells that rang very loudly. If they rang after midnight, it meant either a family crisis or a drunk, marooned on North Hull Estate, had hit the wrong number trying to call a taxi.

On this occasion it was neither. On the line was a man called Tony Fawcett, a factotum working for John Lennon and Yoko. Would I ring John at the following number?

I rang the magic number and heard the famous voice. The message was simple and straightforward: 'Me and Yoko watched your play tonight. We thought it was great. Would you like to come and talk to us about a project?'

We agreed to meet in London later in the week, I hung up and went back to bed.

An hour later the telephone rang again. It was my sister to say my mother had had a heart attack and had been rushed to the Hull Royal Infirmary.

In the hospital, my Mum was pale and wired up to strange devices, but well enough to say she'd enjoyed *Rest in Peace, Uncle Fred*. I'd shared my secret with her: that it was actually about me and Auntie May. She'd understood totally what it was about, without sharing my revolutionary fervour about fixing society to prevent such inequalities corrupting the planet in future. Her attitude was more along the lines of: there there, it'll be all right, pet.

She was also warily impressed by the phone call with John Lennon. To be sure, she liked some of the Beatles music but was baffled by Beatlemania. Her generation had never swooned or screamed over anyone. All that nonsense about Valentino and Sinatra had happened in the States and what else could you expect of Americans?

I was in midstream where the cultural manifestations were concerned. As a Northern boy, I was thrilled that the Beatles were a regional phenomenon. Their songs were about Penny Lane and Strawberry Fields which was a major step forward from nightingales keeping everybody awake in Berkeley Square. Musically they were on the same wavelength as we makers of Wednesday Plays and *Z Cars*.

It was the mania that bothered me. I was a time-served jazz freak and you didn't scream and swoon at jazz concerts. You stayed cool, snapped your finger discreetly on the offbeat and maybe murmured 'Yeah' but only if the word was upon you.

The sixties had liberated the creativity of a lot of people – myself included – but I was married with three young kids, I was doing the school run four times a day, and as far as I was concerned the big sixties rave-up was still happening in the next street and I still wished they'd make less noise.

A couple of days later I took the early morning Hull Pullman for my appointment with John Lennon. I was such a regular on the train I was close to being invited to the British Rail staff dances.

'Where you off to today, our kid?' said the ticket collector after he'd given me a quick analysis of my most recent *Softly Softly* episode. He was very impressed when I told him where I was going.

'Bloody hell, we'll have to start calling you Mr Plater.'

At the Apple building in Harley Street, there were a few kids hanging around outside but one glance told them I wasn't of significance and I was spared the question: 'Are you somebody?' That used to happen all the time outside Granada, where crowds were permanently camped outside, hoping for a glimpse of Ena or Elsie (of *Coronation Street* fame).

In the spirit of the age, it was easy to get in: no security men or numbers to code in. John and Yoko sat behind a big desk in a large office, looking like a pair of under-age Old

Testament prophets. A young man was sitting on the floor in a corner.

'This is me cousin from Liverpool,' said John. 'He's having some pudding. Would you like some?'

Following a split-second internal debate about the relative coolness of accepting or declining pudding, I said yes. Then we got down to business.

John and Yoko had become involved in the case of James Hanratty, who had been hanged in April 1962 for what the papers had dubbed the A6 murder. Various commentators had criticised the case and the verdict at the time, as they do to this day, and along the way John and Yoko had picked up the banner.

'He didn't do it,' said John, 'and we want to make a film saying he didn't do it.'

'Are you going to approach one of the major studios?'

'There'll be none of that crap. This time, I'm the man with the big cigar.'

The main evidence in favour of Hanratty's innocence was a confession from a man called Peter Louis Alphon who at this time was living in Paris. I was given an envelope containing a copy of this confession plus press reports of the original murder and the trial.

I remember a couple of key items about the meeting. The first was Yoko showing me a poem she'd written and asking for my opinion. I recall about twenty words scattered about the page in a fairly random pattern. I also recall saying I was profoundly impressed, too polite to say: there there, it'll be all right, pet.

The other key moment was when I was leaving.

'How much was your train fare?' said John.

'It doesn't matter. Forget it.'

'I asked you to come. I pay your train fare.'

I protested that I was working regularly and earning well, a day return was only a couple of quid and if the cause was a good one, I was always prepared to pay my own train fare.

'We'll call it ten. Then you can have your dinner on the train on the way home.'

And before I left Apple I was given another, smaller envelope containing ten pounds in cash; more than the meal at the Carlton Grill and much more than Auntie May ever earned in a week.

Within the next couple of days I drafted out some preliminary notes on a suggested movie called *Hanratty*. I sent them to John at Apple. Nothing happened for a while. That isn't unusual in the writing trade. The record, as far as I'm aware, is of a play turned down by a fringe theatre seven years after the playwright's death.

But in the interim I telephoned the director, Richard Lester, a good friend from an abandoned project of 1968. I told him the story so far.

'When John says he's the man with the big cigar, should I believe him?' I asked.

'Without question. Whatever John says, you believe him. He's one of the two most original people I've ever met.'

'I hardly dare ask who the other one is.'

'Spike Milligan.'

'Of course.'

Richard obviously caught the merest hint of disappointment in my voice.

'I'm sorry, Alan. You are merely highly talented.'

'Thank you, Richard.'

'But the other thing about John is, by next month he might be equally passionate about something else. And it takes at least two years to make a movie.'

'Are you saying he's got a short concentration span?'

'Pardon?'

The film, *Hanratty*, was never written, let alone made but in the broad sweep of history, it doesn't matter a damn.

Pretty soon, John and Yoko went to live in New York and we all know how that story ended. My Mum died in hospital, ten days after her original heart attack. I was with her at the time. It was the last secret we shared.

I wish you long life.

Rest in Peace, Uncle Fred was my first attempt to integrate jazz – or music of any sort – into the essential fabric of a television play. It was also the last time – possibly the only time – that Tubby Hayes appeared in a play.

This being so, the BBC, with a true sense of history, wiped the tape many years ago.

This is doubly frustrating because there was a little coda to the play that wasn't seen at the time. It should have been but it wasn't. There was a fashion that started in the sixties and continues to this day for a little postscript after the final credits. The Americans call it a sting – a joke, a comment, a wry afterthought.

Because it was a play about class divisions and the state of the nation (some things never change) our coda was a very simple throwaway moment but satirical as Hell. The band is packing up at the end of the gig and the idea was that Tubbs would play one chorus of the National Anthem on vibes and get it slightly wrong. Then, theoretically, the audience would say: 'Wow! What a wonderful, highly-barbed, satirical, nay coruscating comment on the state of the nation.' Or words to that effect.

When we recorded the play Tubbs duly played the National Anthem, as requested, getting it slightly wrong. It worked brilliantly. Unfortunately, when the play was transmitted, the engineers responsible assumed the play was finished when the credits finished and hit the Stop button. Memos had apparently been sent telling them to pay attention and wait until the barb had been transmitted but they either forgot or the memo had gone to the wrong room or they had a headache. We will never know and, in any case, I stopped worrying about it years ago.

It's worth setting the record straight because, according to the work that survived the not-very-selective culling that went on in the drama departments of BBC and ITV, the first time I officially collaborated with musicians on a television play was *The Land of Green Ginger*, made in 1973 in association with my good friends, the Watersons.

Like most of my work, it was a simple enough tale. I've never been heavy on plot and I'm never sure where the stories come from. But in retrospect it's probable that *Green Ginger*'s absolute origins were in a Norma Waterson recording of a traditional song called 'A North Country Maid'. The lyric begins:

> A North Country maid up to London hath strayed
> Although with her nature it did not agree
> And she's wept and she's sighed
> And she's hung her head and cried
> 'How I wish once again in the North I could be'
> Where the oak and the ash and the bonny ivy tree
> All flourish and bloom in my North Country.

The maid in the play is a young woman from Hull, working in London at some vaguely-defined secretarial job, who heads back north, ostensibly to see her mother, but essentially to resolve her relationship with a long-time boyfriend who's a trawlerman. Again, as the song says:

> Well I bet if I pleased I could marry with ease
> For where bonny lasses are lovers will come
> But the lad that I wed
> Must be North Country bred
> And will carry me back to my North Country.

I set the plaintive lyricism of the song in deliberate contrast to the bleaker realities of their situation. The young man has been sailing as first mate on a trawler, but has just got his skipper's ticket. Her dilemma is that she isn't prepared to marry a man whose life will be dominated by three -week-long trips to the fishing grounds off Iceland and Norway, with no guarantee that he'll come back. Hull was still living in the shadow of 1968 when three trawlers – the *Ross Cleveland*, the *St Romanus* and the *Kingston Peridot* – were lost within a ten-day period.

He won't give up the sea. She won't give up her independence. They are both locked into the reality of lives determined by how they make their living. At the end she goes back to London and he goes off to sea in his trawler. Gwen Taylor and John Flanagan gave beautiful, poignant performances but the piece gained additional resonance from the music: a selection of love songs, shanties and drinking songs from the Watersons' vast memory bank of traditional songs. We also saw them giving a live performance at the Haworth Arms pub, almost my favourite moment in the film.

To this day, most music in film and television tends to be called – with total accuracy – 'incidental'. It underlines the moments – scary bits, sad bits, look-behind-you bits. It tells the watchers what they should be thinking and, more important, feeling, all too often on the assumption that they're too stupid to work it out for themselves.

In *Land of Green Ginger*, as in *Rest in Peace, Uncle Fred*, the music did more than this. It not only reflected the action, it helped to generate and inspire the action. Instead of being glued on afterwards, it was written into the script more or less from the first draft stage. The music – as the critic Chris Dunkley has pointed out – became a character in the drama.

I don't claim to be unique in this respect. Can we imagine *The Third Man* without the Anton Karas zither? Or Truffaut's *Tirez sur le pianiste* without that wonderful piano theme by Georges Delerue. And Woody Allen's entire film-making career can be seen as a homage to the music – and especially the jazz – that has done so much to illuminate his days and nights, and ours.

Examples in television are thinner on the ground, with the notable exception of Dennis Potter's work; and there's no doubt that, in the 1970s, the field was wide open for adventures in new ways of making drama.

One of the adventures that beckoned me with a tempting finger was lyric-writing.

In 1968 I had written a stage show called *Close the Coalhouse Door*, a musical about the history of the Durham miners. I didn't do it on my own. The stories came from the Newcastle-based, Shildon-born novelist and short story writer, Sid Chaplin, who had started his working life down the pit.

The songs were written by Alex Glasgow, a Gateshead man, a singer and song-maker with a lovely ear for melody and a unique ability to blend lyricism and rage in a four-line stanza.

The show played to packed houses in Newcastle and a year later reached London's West End by way of Nottingham Playhouse. The critics voted it the best musical of the year and hardly anybody came to see it. Over the years I've met most of them. Astonishingly, the campaign to keep it running was headed by the *Sun* newspaper, in its pre-Murdoch days, and its theatre critic, David Nathan. I didn't know at the time that David was a dedicated keeper of the jazz flame and there was certainly no jazz in *Coalhouse Door* – but no doubt there was an underlying jazz attitude in the show, notably a scepticism about governments and an enduring love of the commonfolk.

Alex was lukewarm about jazz but he was passionate about songs and singers, especially the European chansonniers like Brel and Brassens. He and Jake Thackray – both accomplished linguists – once spent an entire evening trying to work out the joke in a verse of a Brassens song before agreeing that the line in question was sung in French, but with a Belgian accent. The accent made it funny.

When writing *Coalhouse Door* our method (these days it would be called 'methodology') was very simple – almost naive. When I thought a song was appropriate I would write some lyrics, very quickly and badly, indicating the dramatic intention of the number. As long as the intention was clear, it didn't matter that the words were naff. Alex would read them, get the message, burn my lyrics and do the whole job properly.

Over a period, an unspoken challenge began to take shape. The challenge was to write lyrics for Alex that were so good he didn't need to change them. Progress was slow. A couple of lines might survive. Then maybe a whole verse. The ultimate triumph came when I wrote a series called *Trinity Tales* for BBC television.

This was an updated version of Chaucer's *Canterbury Tales*. In the original, a motley collection of travellers makes a pilgrimage with spiritual overtones and on the way they tell each other stories. Our modern parallel was a group of Rugby League supporters going to Wembley (old Wembley, obviously, with the towers) for the Cup Final to cheer on their team, Trinity.

This seems to me a major element that went wrong in the 2003 BBC take on Chaucer. A series of one-off plays, there was no over-arching journey therefore no overall developing narrative. I won't make any other invidious comparisons though some other people did at the time.

I subjected the original characters to a fairly broad update. The Friar became Stan the Fryer, who has a fish-and-chip shop and the Wife of Bath became the Wife of Batley. That gives a fair idea of the style of the series: rough and ready, coarse and tender, and – crucially – with original songs and music.

I set myself a challenge: to write a set of lyrics that Alex would be unable to resist. I took the chance in the context of a story about a de facto seven stone weakling, a species of humanity for whom I've always had great affection: men in early middle-age, fundamentally incapable of doing any harm if only because they're incapable of doing anything at all, aside from collecting train numbers, making models of cathedrals out of used matches or – let's be honest – knowing the full details of all Charlie Parker's false starts and out-takes. According to the good book, eventually these men will inherit the earth, but it's been a long wait for most of them.

They have to settle for being recurring characters in many of my plays.

In *Trinity Tales* he was played by Francis Matthews – the same actor who had starred as the brave, resourceful and exceedingly handsome Paul Temple in the Francis Durbridge television series. The transformation was easily achieved by means of a flat cap, thick spectacles, a long belted raincoat and a tendency to bump into things.

For reasons of plot – don't blame me, blame Geoffrey Chaucer – he falls helplessly in love with a beautiful, rich, blonde, statuesque woman played by Gaye Brown. She sets him an apparently impossible challenge: if he can win a place in the Great Britain Rugby League team she will give herself to him.

'Come to my house wearing your international cap and you may do with me what you will.'

He goes to the local Rugby League ground and volunteers his services. He is laughed at by large men. But then the miracle happens. His glasses fall off, are trodden on by one of the large men, played by Bill Maynard, and he is transformed. Without his glasses he can kick goals with a fluency and precision that Jonny Wilkinson could only look on with envy. Without his glasses he is a genius of Rugby League. Without his glasses he wins his international cap.

He returns to the big house, wearing the cap, and she gives way.

'Come to bed,' she says.

'But I'm not tired,' he says. 'I'd rather go to the pictures.'

And that's where we see them for the last time, on their way to see *Casablanca*.

In a 2005 poll, the 1970s were voted the best television decade of our time and while accepting that democracy comes up with some very funny answers, it's also arguable that for television dramatists it was the best of times – if only because we could get away with stuff like this. We could also get away with songs and music.

The lyrics I wrote for my seven stone weakling were titled 'Plain Song' and started something like this:

> Won't anybody love a plain man?
> Won't anybody feel the pain?
> I'm beset by fear of the female sex
> Though passion's steaming up my specs
> Won't anybody learn to love a man who's plain?

I posted the complete lyrics to Alex in Gateshead. They arrived by the first post the next day and he telephoned me around lunchtime and sang the song to me. That was another characteristic of the period. Though we had no faxes or emails, everything happened very quickly. At my *Z Cars* peak I would deliver a script and it would be transmitted live six weeks later. Nowadays it takes six weeks to organise a lunch date or to have someone return your phone call. This isn't an old man's fanciful remembrance, but accurate reportage. We have lost one of the most precious gifts a writer can possess: the shortest possible route to the audience.

It was in these faraway, innocent times that I became increasingly intoxicated by the experience of writing lyrics and started a new imaginary scrapbook of heroes in the sphere: Cole Porter, Ira Gershwin, Lorenz Hart and Johnny Mercer. In *Kiss Me Kate*, Porter wrote a stanza for the song 'Always True to You in My Fashion' that runs:

> Mr Harris, plutocrat
> Wants to give my cheek a pat
> If a Harris pat means a Paris hat – hooray!
> But I'm always true to you, darling, in my fashion
> I'm always true to you, darling, in my way.

That Harris pat/Paris hat inversion fills me with almost as much awe and wonder as any of Shakespeare's sonnets. Much the same applies to Ira Gershwin's lyric for 'The Lorelei' and the couplet:

> She had a most immoral eye
> That's why they called her Lorelei...

One of the finest lyrics ever must be Johnny Mercer's version of 'When the World Was Young': total perfection from beginning to end, and not a syllable out of place.

They were the major players in a game I was dealing into. The sensible thing was to do so in a small, though not all that quiet, corner: specifically the Bush Theatre on Shepherds Bush Green in London.

For years Bill Tidy had delighted readers of the *Daily Mirror* with his cartoon strip, *The Fosdyke Saga*. Inspired, at some considerable distance, by Galsworthy's *Forsyte Saga*, it told the story of the Fosdyke family, founders of a mighty tripe dynasty with roots in Griddlesbury, Lancashire, who then move on to Manchester prior to taking over the world. Mike Bradwell, founder of the Hull Truck Theatre Company, invited me to do a stage version – a task defined by Bill as 'glueing my balloons together.'

The play, and its sequel, *Fosdyke 2* – a response to over-whelming public demand for more – both opened at the Bush before touring up and down the land. For a while the Fosdyke shows became something of a cult. A fine Hull poet called John Robinson, scion of a real-life tripe manu-facturing company, organised a special range of tinned tripe, obtainable at all the major touring venues. There were serious discussions about organising an annual

Fosdyke Mystery Cycle but then the bar closed and we forgot about it.

The two shows had qualities unique, to the best of my knowledge and experience, in the history of Western European theatre. Never before or since has an audience been pelted with tripe by the actors, and specifically invited to throw it back at the actors. To be sure, there have been many examples down the ages of audiences throwing all manner of things at performers but this was the only time the ammunition was supplied by members of the cast.

We also had our own anthem, which the audience was expected to join in, with intimidation if necessary. As a piece of lyric-writing, it was a long way removed from Ira Gershwin and Lorenz Hart, but it has its own unique qualities. The scene is the Bush Theatre, an intimate room above a pub, so intimate that a hamster would feel claustrophobic, with seats so uncomfortable that I once accused the management of taking commission from all the osteopaths in north London. The audience is standing up, being careful not to skid on the assorted slivers of tripe that litter the auditorium.

And solemnly they sing:

Fosdykes Arise
Fosdykes Arise
Lift up thine eyes
See the Fosdykes Arise

Tripe it is grand
Tripe it is noble
In every land
Tripe it is global

Better by far
Than fowl, fish or weevil
Let there be tripe
And banish all evil

Fosdykes Arise
Fosdykes Arise
Lift up thine eyes
See the Fosdykes arise.

The stage direction then reads: 'Repeat and repeat until everybody has *almost* had enough, then stop.'

The music for the Fosdyke shows was written by Bernard Wrigley, a totally remarkable actor/singer/comedian/renaissance man from Bolton, Lancashire. Among many other properties he has a deep voice – his folk club billing is the Bolton Bullfrog – and a keen sense of the people's history embracing everything from traditional folk songs to jazz, music-hall and comic monologues. He is also a player and specialist collector of concertinas and has a wonderful ear for the music of everyday speech. One of his songs is a comment on the funny way people speak in Blackburn, which is all of six miles distant from Bolton. One of their peculiarities, apparently, is their pronunciation of the word 'car' and 'cur' – thus Bernard's song is all about 'purking curs in the curpurk'.

These things can only happen in the North of England and must be treasured at all costs.

There was an odd sequel to our song-writing partnership. Paul McCartney's brother, Mike, approached us with a proposition. Would Bernard and I like to do a version of the anthem suitable for recording by The Scaffold, of which he was a founder-member? This would involve making the words a little more universal, we decided.

The final stanza of the revised version ran:

Tripe it is grand
Tripe it is noble
In every land
Tripe it is global
Blessed are the meek
For they'll find salvation
When nations speak
Tripe unto nation
Fosdykes Arise...
Etc.

In the event, The Scaffold proposal never materialised but Bernard sang the new version on his LP, *Ten Ton Special*, accompanied by the Owd Platting Lane Band from Rochdale, recorded live at the Middleton Civic Hall.

Mike Bradwell's comment was: 'I liked it better with the weevils.' But I realised that I'd fulfilled an ambition. The composer credit on the album reads: Wrigley-Tidy-Plater. I was right up there with De Sylva, Brown and Henderson.

We are all creatures of fashion, whether we like it or not. In the fifties we proclaimed our non-conformity by stamping our feet in unison to the Humphrey Lyttelton band; in the seventies, even those aging rebels became obliged to acknowledge that the rock revolution wasn't going away. Some of us, for a while, signed up as associate members.

This is a roundabout way of confessing that in 1978 I worked on a rock musical, though in mitigation I can only point out that everybody was at it.

It wasn't my idea. This is a recurring theme in my career. Many of the shows that feature on Alan's Greatest Hits album – *Fortunes of War, Barchester Chronicles, A Very British Coup* – weren't my idea. I was just the hired hand.

This time the idea came from David Rose, probably the greatest television drama producer of our time. He masterminded the early *Z Cars* series before moving to Birmingham with the very BBC title, Head of Drama (English Regions), where he made network television available to a huge array of dangerous young talent, from Alan Bleasdale to Mike Leigh.

David was totally fearless. He had flown bombing missions during the war, and that being so, a strongly-worded memo from a channel controller was never going to frighten him. One of his favourite methods was to take a couple of people from different areas of the business, throw them together and see what happened. He did this with me and Dave Greenslade.

Dave was, and is, a keyboard player of enormous talent, though difficult to categorise. A long-time member of Colosseum, along with Jon Hiseman and the late Dick Heckstall-Smith, he operates in the area generally classified as jazz/rock. He's also, to quote one of my own plays, 'a sweet guy and a very dear friend'.

The offer from David Rose was irresistible: 'If you two get along, make a musical.' Well, we did and we did. One of our meetings was in Dave's shed at the bottom of his garden, where he stored all manner of keyboards, synthesizers, vibes and electronic gadgetry. He was able to summon up all manner of amazing sounds, including the Vienna Boys Choir. I was entranced by it all though I did ask, after Dave played me a very impressive trumpet solo on keyboard: 'That's all very well, but can you give me Cootie Williams?'

The plots of all plays, from the Greeks onwards, sound a bit silly when you describe them, but this one was sillier than most. The piece was eventually called *Curriculee Curricula* but its working title was *Spanners Across the Campus*, which I still prefer.

A young workman called Benny turns up at a university in search of a bag of spanners which he mislaid while doing some maintenance work. He is confronted by a series of increasingly eccentric academics who have never heard of spanners, he falls in love with a pretty girl, and they end up wrecking the graduation ceremony in the grand hall. Chris Farlowe played Benny, Sonja Kristina played the pretty girl and there was a guest appearance by Patrick Moore, though it would take too long to explain why.

The whole thing was amiably over the top: the story, the action and Alastair Reid's anarchic direction, complete with superimposed bubbles bearing words like 'CRASH!' and 'POW!' Musically I can only recall bits and pieces. Benny's opening song, as he rides his motor-bike on to the campus, was a cheerful number starting:

> My name is Benny and I ain't got many
> Ideas in my head
> But to make me some bread
> And keep the wolf away from the old front door

Dave agreed this was right on the money, funk-wise, though we never used language of that kind.

I also wrote a homage to W. S. Gilbert with a song for the Vice-Chancellor beginning:

> We are the very model of a modern university
> We specialise in truth and lies and every known perversity. . .

Dave set that one in a big band swing arrangement, in the course of which he paid his homage to the great Oliver

Nelson. What's more, I think he did it without leaving his shed.

It wasn't the only sign that the times they were a-changing. After the graduation ceremony had been wrecked, Dave's band took to the stage for what, in effect, was a live gig. The students (real-live Birmingham university students pretending to be fictional students) all stood up and rushed down to the stage, hands held high above their heads, clapping along with the music. Nobody asked them to do it. It was a genuine, spontaneous reaction.

Dave explained to me later that this was what happened on a good night at rock concerts.

'We used to stamp our feet to Humph,' I said, 'but we'd stay in our seats to do it. We sat in neat rows.'

'That was then. This is now.'

I still see Dave from time to time and we re-affirm our intention that we should work together again. Twenty-seven years after *Curriculee Curricula* we still haven't given up on the idea.

When I look back at my three main collaborators from that period – Alex Glasgow, Bernard Wrigley and Dave Greenslade – the thing they have in common is that they can't be categorised. They're like those awkward prizes handed out at Awards ceremonies: the ones usually edited out of the television coverage. Best Short Film Not in the English Language; Lifetime Achievement in Sub-titling; Best Supporting Accountant in a Musical.

Alex, especially, loathed categories. He was a song-maker with a lovely voice and though he recorded traditional material, he was no lover of the folk scene. 'You get some bugger with his finger in his ear, singing about being a shepherd and he's never seen a bloody sheep in his life.'

Bernard, in a way, embraces all categories. A generation or two earlier, he'd have worked the music-halls. In his work you can hear George Formby, father and son, but you can also hear an essentially Bolton variety of the blues.

And Dave, both personally and musically, is probably too gentle to be a true rocker. He's long been called 'the quiet man of rock' and there's certainly an enduring lyrical quality to his fusing of elements from all over the aural landscape. In his shed there are many mansions.

Looking back, it's clear that I was still skirting around the edges of jazz in my work; but that was about to change, courtesy Duke Ellington, Bix Beiderbecke and, curiously enough, J. B. Priestley.

Blue Note

If there was a single jazz record label that crystallised the spirit of the 1970s, and the kind of music I was listening to then, it had to be Blue Note. Even if you didn't like the music, the sleeves were works of art, and there was lots of information. Jazz fans feed on information, though we all remember when it used to be called education.

This is a song of celebration.

> Blue Note
> Is the place to be
> Blue Note
> Is the place for me
> If you like your music blue and funky
> If you like your piano playing clunky
> Just send a message with your flunkey
> To Blue Note
>
> Blue Note
> Take it on LP
> Blue Note
> Never on CD
> If your faith in trad is sort of shaky
> And you figure free-form's kind of flakey
> You'll restore your soul with Mister Blakey
> On Blue Note
>
> Blue Note
> Is the very top
> Blue Note
> Is the land of bop
> If you find Bing Crosby too harmonious

And you fancy flattened fifths euphonious
Then your ears are waiting for Thelonious
On Blue Note

Blue Note
It will blow your mind
Blue Note
Is the place to find
Just how Horace Silver can achieve notes
Clifford playing like-you-won't-believe-notes
And you'll educate yourself with sleeve notes
From Blue Note

Blue Note
Is the very end
Blue Note
Will be your best friend
Say goodbye to Songs for Swinging Lovers
Not to mention Hendrix and the Mothers
Screw the music – dig those LP covers
On Blue Note

5.

Dear Bix

My journey into jazz on television wasn't planned. It was a series of interlocking accidents and coincidences, many of them of a kind that couldn't happen in today's middle-management dominated culture.

In 1980 I wrote a drama serial based on J. B. Priestley's most famous novel, *The Good Companions*, for Yorkshire Television. It's a backstage story about a touring concert party and an uncompromising feel-good yarn about what the Americans used to call happy people with happy problems.

We did it as a full-blooded musical. In the true MGM tradition, the characters sang, danced and generally pranced around. They pranced the length of the pier in Llandudno and on the platforms of the railway station in Keighley, beloved location of all film-makers in search of period travelling. If they were happy, they sang about it. If they were sad, they also sang about it, but in a minor key.

The music was written by David Fanshawe. He won't mind if I describe him as a bit of an eccentric. For years he travelled extensively around Africa and the Middle East, recording ethnic music and assorted ambient sounds. He then integrated the recordings into vast orchestral and choral works, notably *African Sanctus* which probably remains his greatest hit. He once conducted a performance of the *Sanctus* at the Albert Hall in full explorer costume of khaki shirt, shorts, sensible boots and pith helmet. He was never going to be confused with Alex Glasgow, Bernard Wrigley or Dave Greenslade.

We set to work. I said to David: 'All we have to do is write "Night and Day" and we've cracked it.' We never did. To give ourselves the benefit of many a doubt, the series was interesting but flawed, and didn't really catch on. The opening episode was blasted out of the water by most of the critics, including a panel on BBC TV's *Did You See?*

I wrote exceedingly angry letters to the panellists, one of whom was Larry Adler. He replied, quoting, with considerable relish, some of his own lousy reviews, and on the basis of that correspondence we became lifelong friends.

What went wrong? Looking back, it's clear we all had too good a time. I'm a great believer in the principle that work should be fun, but the enjoyment should embrace the audience. Sometimes the good time becomes exclusive to the play-makers. We sing the song but we don't invite the audience to join in the chorus.

I think we all became intoxicated by our own cleverness. I'd fallen in love with convoluted triple-rhyming schemes, which probably didn't do David any favours, not to mention the actors who had to wrap their voices around my verbal cuteness. Having preached about 'Tea for Two' I didn't heed my own advice. Apparently Lester Young, towards the end of his life, played a gig with a young tearaway tenor player of the hundred-notes-a-minute school.

Afterwards Lester said to him: 'You sure play a lot of notes, but lady, what's your story?'

Too many words – that was the problem. I'd post them to David with a sort of Eric and Ernie attitude: 'Get out of that.' In fairness, some of the numbers were quite jolly but when I can bear to play the LP – which, to Yorkshire Television's chagrin, didn't exactly sell in millions – I cringe at one or two of the items. Parodies of early Benjamin Britten were never likely to make the charts.

There wasn't any jazz in our score. The only glance in that direction was a song in Episode One, called 'The Original Bruddesford Dixieland Ragtime Band', sung by a couple of young lads off to the local dance-hall. Larry really hated that song. For lovers of the truly pedantic and peculiar, the trumpet player on that track is Kenny Baker. But none of this explains how J. B. Priestley nudged me towards jazz on television. This involves a prequel.

When David Cunliffe, then Yorkshire TV's Head of Drama, first approached me about *The Good Companions*, he wanted it in thirteen episodes. Historically, television has always worked in sixes, sevens and thirteens, which, properly organised, eventually add up to fifty-two, that being the number of weeks in a year.

I read the book and told David it didn't need thirteen episodes.

'Thirteen is too many. I can do it in nine.'

'So what do we do for the other four weeks?' he said.

'Easy. I'll write you a four-part original. I fancy doing a non-violent thriller.'

'Deal,' said David.

Problem solved. As I keep saying, they were innocent days.

The four-part original was called *Get Lost!* The idea came

from a newspaper item. It said that according to official records, twenty thousand people disappeared every year. I think that was the number. It might have been more, but whichever way you looked at it, it was a lot of people and a lot of unexplained disappearances.

It seemed a good basis for a mystery: an organisation, complete with a Mr X, organising, for a modest fee, the disappearance of people who've had enough of whatever life they're currently leading.

So much for the mystery. Now I needed some investigators – a pair of amateur detectives in the great tradition of Holmes and Watson, except my chosen models were Nick and Norah Charles of the great *Thin Man* movies. Knowing that we'd be shooting the series in and around Leeds, I asked a simple question. Where would be the least likely place to find such a pair? Answer: in the staffroom of a state comprehensive school. And who would they be? Answer: he would be Mr Keaton, a jazz fanatic who taught woodwork and she would be Mrs Threadgold, a political activist who taught English. The publicity material carried the billing: 'They were not brave. They were not beautiful. But they were available.'

If all this bears a striking resemblance to the *Beiderbecke Trilogy*, there's a very simple explanation: in embryo, *Get Lost!* was actually *Beiderbecke* waiting to be born.

We just hadn't got there yet.

The springboard for the plot is the disappearance of Mrs Threadgold's husband. She doesn't particularly want him back. She simply wants to know where he's gone, and why. She's looking for closure though – praise be – that word hadn't entered everyone's vocabulary in 1981.

Mr Keaton comes to her aid. Over the course of four episodes they solve the mystery and fall in something closely resembling love.

I added two additional ingredients to the mix. The first was a continuing voice-over narrative after the manner of the great Raymond Chandler. Thus, when their search took them to the seaside resorts of the Yorkshire coast, we heard Keaton saying things like: 'It was seven, maybe eight in the evening, when we headed down the mean streets on the lower East Side of downtown Bridlington. We checked out the off-licences, the takeaways and the fish-and-chip shops. There was salt in our hair and vinegar in our nostrils. The weather was cold and bleak and so were the people. You could die on these streets but nobody would shed a tear, unless you paid them scale with a little extra on the top for sincerity.'

Screenwriters can do this stuff by the yard and it takes a resolute producer to stop them.

The other ingredient was the music. Since our unbrave, unbeautiful but available hero was a jazz fan, obsessed with Duke Ellington – no surprise there – we opted for a score in the ducal tradition. Keith Morgan, the head of music at Yorkshire Television, recommended a young guy called Frank Ricotti, a percussionist and vibes player who, as some sort of youthful prodigy in north London, had been the inspiration for what eventually became the National Youth Jazz Orchestra.

Frank did an impeccable job. The main theme for the series was Ellington's 'Dual Highway', a lazy, relaxed, laid-back number that sounds as if it arrived in the recording studio ready-made on the back of an envelope. Working from this basis, Frank then developed all manner of themes and variations, within the Ellington small-group tradition.

Kenny Baker doubled for Cootie Williams or Ray Nance, according to the demands of the score, and I'm pretty sure Don Lusher was the officially-designated Lawrence Brown.

Though we were only scratching the surface, it was *Get Lost!* that made me aware of the possibilities of jazz in relation to the kind of drama I write. That's a vital qualification: I don't think jazz would work in the same way for, say, Samuel Beckett or Harold Pinter. But there are qualities in my work – and, I guess, in my view of the world – also found in jazz and the people who make the music: suspicion of authority, a taste for bleak jokes, respect for eccentricity, a reluctance to wear a tie, and a love of people who only flourish and bloom after dark.

Someone told me that on a visit to England during the 1960s, Duke Ellington asked a journalist: 'Who is your prime minister?'

'Harold Wilson,' he was told.

'This man Wilson – is he one of the day people or the night people?'

'Definitely one of the day people.'

At this point Duke changed the subject.

One of my favourite sequences in *Get Lost!* was one where the pictures-plus-music started to make a whole new brand of sense. It was a car chase, the only one I've ever written.

When writing a caper of this kind, I take guidance from Dr Samuel Johnson, not that he was an expert on car chases; but he once defined art as old delights presented in a new way or new delights presented in an old way.

Applying this principle to car chases means if you are going to have one, remember the audience has seen every example from *The Keystone Cops* to *The French Connection*. Therefore, be damn sure you do it in a new way.

I did it – if you'll pardon the expression – my way. Having checked out the fish-and-chip shops, Keaton and Threadgold mosey on down the Yorkshire coast to a caravan site where – for reasons of the enigmatic plot – they have to chase a car driven by the bad guy. However, like most caravan sites, there is a speed limit: in this case, 10 m.p.h., a speed limit which both drivers observe.

The other problem with a car chase is how to end it. The Hollywood solutions include a) the good guy crashes and the bad guy gets away, though this only happens in the middle of the movie; b) the bad guy crashes and is killed, though this obviously happens towards the end of the movie, just before the hero drives on to the airport and intercepts the girl just as she's about to take a plane out of his life forever, or c) everybody crashes, as in *The Blues Brothers* – which, for the record, remains my favourite car chase.

The solution in *Get Lost!* was simpler and, inevitably with a television budget, cheaper. Mr Keaton, the good guy, runs out of petrol. Why? Because the bad guy has siphoned the petrol out of his tank. Steve McQueen never thought of that.

The series was well liked and I was commissioned to write a sequel. It was called *Get Lost Revisited*. Then we hit problems. Alun Armstrong and Bridget Turner had played the lead roles but in the interim Alun had landed a plum part in the Royal Shakespeare Company's production of *Nicholas Nickleby* and was on his way to Broadway. David Cunliffe summoned me to a crisis meeting.

'What are we going to do?' he said.

'I could burst into tears,' I said.

'Any other ideas?'

'Or I could revamp the scripts, give it a new title and we

could cast two different actors.'

'Name one,' said David.

'James Bolam,' I said.

There are very few guaranteed ways of getting your work on television but the name, James Bolam, is one. From *The Likely Lads* to *New Tricks* he has long demonstrated his ability to deliver an audience. His secret is very simple: he's a great actor.

He read the scripts, said yes, and *The Beiderbecke Trilogy* was on its way.

One day in 1985 a man went into a record shop and asked the woman if they had any LPs by Bix Beiderbecke.

'We've sold out,' she said. 'I blame that television series.'

It was an early example of the Beiderbecke phenomenon. It wasn't a tidal wave that swamped the musical cosmos but it was a significant ripple. There was a revival of interest in Bix's music and in the work of Kenny Baker, who replicated the Beiderbecke sound for the benefit of the series.

People assumed, wrongly, that Bix was my ultimate jazz hero. It wasn't the case and still isn't. If I were to drift into anorak mode and make a Top Ten list, he probably wouldn't be on it.

Let's try it. Duke Ellington, Louis Armstrong, Jelly Roll Morton, Johnny Hodges, Lester Young, Dizzy Gillespie, Charlie Parker, Billie Holiday, Ella Fitzgerald, Charles Mingus.

No, he doesn't make the list. Sorry Bix.

That being so, why call it *The Beiderbecke Affair* in the first place? It isn't a complicated answer. I just liked the sound of his name. The title scans nicely and makes sweet music.

It did involve having a line of explanation in each of the

series, clarifying who he was for the benefit of the 95 per cent of the audience who wouldn't know Bix from a Twix.

In the first episode of the *Affair*, Trevor Chaplin, the jazz-crazed woodwork teacher formerly known as Neville Keaton, tells us all we need to know.

'Bix Beiderbecke, the first great white jazz musician. Born in Davenport, Iowa, he drank himself to death. His playing sounded like bullets shot from a bell.'

In the first episode of the *Tapes*, the second Beiderbecke series, Jill Swinburne, formerly known as Mrs Threadgold, repeats the speech word for word. This astonishes Trevor.

'How did you know that?' he says.

'You gave me a twenty-minute lecture about it in bed one night. In lieu of the cigarette.'

'I never knew you listened when I talked.'

If the change from Keaton to Chaplin was fairly obvious, if only to students of silent film comedy, the Threadgold-to-Swinburne development was a little more abstruse. I've been waiting years for someone to ask for an explanation, but so far nobody has. Let me explain it anyway. They were both names of largely-forgotten goalkeepers. Harry Threadgold played for Sunderland and Tommy Swinburne played for Newcastle United.

James Bolam transformed Trevor Chaplin into one of the most remarkable anti-heroes of our time, but he would be the first to acknowledge Barbara Flynn as an equal and, in most ways, opposite partner.

Barbara had played a relatively small part in *Barchester Chronicles*, my Anthony Trollope dramatisation and I had been deeply impressed not only by her acting, but by her remarkable Donald Duck impersonations. When her name was suggested to play Jill Swinburne I said: 'Get her. At once. Put the cheque in the post.'

Though the series made a more or less immediate impact, the name Beiderbecke gave some people trouble, both in the spelling and the pronunciation. One good friend always referred to Bix as Baedeker, presumably confusing him with Karl of that name, a German publisher (1801–59) who is generally credited with inventing guidebooks.

We gave our friend some Beiderbecke records but it did no good. Maybe we should have given her some guidebooks.

In any case, it was never my intention to stick with the name Beiderbecke throughout the three series. According to my screenwriter's masterplan, the second series was to be called *The Gillespie Tapes* and dedicated to Dizzy, and the third series was to be *The Yardbird Suite*, in honour of Charlie Parker. However, the then head of Yorkshire Television, Paul Fox, said: 'We've spent a lot of time and money teaching the audience how to recognise the name Beiderbecke. I don't see why we should start all over again.'

Beiderbecke it remained and, over the years, it became what the marketing gurus would call a brand image. Over and above the music, it symbolised a parallel universe, set in the moonstruck outer limits of Leeds, where only the bizarre was commonplace. When asked by journalists to define what sort of writer I was, I coined the phrase 'gritty northern surrealist.' It seems to fit comfortably enough.

It also seemed to fit our audience's perception of the world. I lost count of the teachers who said to me: 'Our school is just like San Quentin High,' and Sergeant (later Inspector) Hobson, our amiably inept graduate copper, fast-tracking his way through the ranks, produced endless reactions from within the force, along the lines of: 'We've got one just like him.'

Needless to say, the springboard for many of the tales was simple observation. During my years in Hull, a group of writers, poets and musicians would do occasional evenings of 'Poetry and Music' around the city and the East Riding, generally for good causes. I don't remember money ever changing hands though we were never too proud to accept free beer. The billing was either 'Poetry and Folk', 'Poetry and Jazz' or, on one occasion, 'Poetry and Flamenco'. Poets were always more freely available than musicians in Hull, a phenomenon embracing everyone from Andrew Marvell to Philip Larkin and Douglas Dunn. It must be something in the water.

My favourite musical companions were Carol Mills, a teacher who sang a mean blues and an impressive range of dirty songs, and an extraordinary double-act called Sid and Norm. Sid Clark was a clerk with British Railways and Norman Beedle was an advertising copywriter by trade, who in his spare time wrote gags for Bob Monkhouse, and Ken Dodd. Sid and Norm played little ukeleles which they carried onstage in supermarket carrier bags and wrote much of their own material, including such gems as the 'Take Your Hand Off My Whippet Blues' and 'Take Me Back Where I Belong to Dear Old Wetwang'. Wetwang, for the geographically uninformed, is a real village in the East Riding of Yorkshire.

Sid and Norm were both brought up on Hessle Road, the old working-class area of the city where, by tradition, the fishing community lived. Norman recalled, as a child, seeing a cat lying on a side of ham in the window of the Co-op but, as he said, 'it was washing itself at the time.'

One evening we were booked to appear at the church hall in Little Weighton, a village to the west of the city. We arrived early and went for a drink in the local pub. As we started to drink, the sound of Oscar Peterson filled the bar. I checked with the barman.

'Is that Oscar Peterson?'

'The one and only.'

'I don't think I've ever heard Oscar Peterson in a pub.'

'It's strictly against regulations. I'm supposed to play official music supplied by the brewery, but it's all crap so I always play my own tapes in the early evening before the place fills up.'

Aficionados will recognise this as the key opening scene of *The Beiderbecke Tapes*, except in the series the barman is playing Bix rather than Oscar.

The first sign that we were on to something special, musically speaking, happened one day at the recording studio. Frank Ricotti and the guys were doing the music for the second series and during the lunch break a journalist from a jazz magazine came in to interview Kenny Baker and me, in that order. I was sitting in a corner, waiting my turn, and realised that Kenny was describing, in great and precise detail, the first series.

Bear in mind we were working with the top session musicians in the business: Kenny, Don Lusher, Allan Ganley and others of that ilk, who spent much of their working life playing dots for fifty-seven varieties of movies, television shows and commercials. They would do the job brilliantly but, in general, that was it. Once they left the studio, they forgot all about it. With *Beiderbecke*, an amazing truth started to emerge: they watched the show and, not only that, they were fans. For me it was truly a Wow! moment.

In addition, the world outside ('the real world' as people sometimes call it, though I don't know why, let alone what it means) was beginning to take notice. In 1986, Frank was nominated for a BAFTA award for his *Beiderbecke*

Affair music. Unfortunately this coincided with Yorkshire
Television blacking the awards because of a perceived bias
in the nominations towards BBC programmes. I rang
Frank.

'Does that mean they won't buy you a couple of tickets
for the ceremony?'

'Yes.'

'So what happens if you win? Are you going to wait outside and wander in off the street?'

'It's not a problem. I'm playing in the band so I'll be
there anyway.'

'That's cool.'

It would have been very special – one for the archives –
to see a BAFTA winner making his way to the stage from
the bandstand but sadly, Frank didn't win and it didn't
happen.

There was a happier sequel two years later when Frank
won the award for *The Beiderbecke Tapes* music but on that
occasion he was sitting at a table in the Grosvenor House
among civilians and the wreckage of supper.

The process of making all three series was amazingly casual. I had been commissioned to write the third series, *The
Beiderbecke Connection*, and was in that pre-brooding stage,
trying to decide what to put in it, when one night
we dropped in to Ronnie Scott's. Frank was playing in a
backing band for Madeline Bell and during one of the
breaks we had a conversation that ran:

'We're doing another *Beiderbecke* series. Important question, Frank. Is there anything you haven't done musically
that you'd like to do this time?'

I guess at the back of my mind was the thought that,
having been tied down to the Beiderbecke convention, he
might relish being let off the lead for a free-range gallop in

the direction of anybody from Mingus to Mahler. Total freedom of artistic expression and all that jazz, so to speak.

He gave serious thought to the proposition and came up with the answer.

'It would be nice to be in the picture.'

With this one line he gave me the bones of an entire episode of the *Connection*, when Trevor and Jill spend an evening at a newly opened jazz club, based in the singing room of a pub called the Limping Whippet. The club is run by an amiably eccentric character called Mr Pitt, who appears in all three series. In the first he is a hapless official at the town hall; in the second, a totally inept registrar of births, deaths and marriages ('It was a career move. I took lateral promotion at less money,' he explains); and in the third he has been down-sized and is using his redundancy money to run his own jazz club.

'Once a week on Thursdays. I've calculated the money will run out after a month but it should be a good month.'

He was played, memorably, by Robert Longden, himself a jazz fan, who wrote and produced a musical play called *Pretty for the People*, about Louis Prima, which shone briefly but brightly on London's theatrical fringe in the early 1990s.

On the night, in the series, he preens in front of the audience, wearing an ill-fitting tuxedo, and announces:

'Ladies and gentlemen, the Limping Whippet is proud to present, direct from London, England, the Frank Ricotti All-Stars!'

And that's how drama is made.

Frank also had a line to speak. After Trevor has regaled him, in the manner of jazz anoraks the world over, with a detailed catalogue of all the times he's heard him play, the records he's made, complete with an analysis and assessment of his alternate takes, Frank comments: 'That's cool.'

I've always had a soft spot for harmless obsessives and people who follow their dreams, preferably wacky ones. Such a man was Brian Hainsworth, a sweet guy who, following retirement from the textile industry, started a record label called Dormouse. Initially he reissued albums by British bands of the fifties, including Freddie Randall, Ken Colyer and the Crane River Band. He then approached Yorkshire Television about the *Beiderbecke* music. It emerged they had no plans to do anything with it, possibly because they still had a warehouse stacked high with unsold LPs of *The Good Companions* music. Their reaction was, more or less: 'Take it, it's yours.'

Brian produced *The Beiderbecke Collection* which, to everyone's surprise and delight, became a best-seller, if only by the modest standards of jazz. It won a disc of some sort – gold, silver, platinum or possibly EPNS – but enough to make us all very happy for him and the music. I've had many good career moments but few to match hearing Humph, on his Monday night radio programme, announcing: 'The Frank Ricotti All-Stars playing... Live at the Limping Whippet.'

Beiderbecke attracted a deal of what I have to call fan mail. It wasn't a totally new experience, though the letters had never amounted to a flood. They were more of an occasional drip building up to a trickle if a piece of work was particularly well liked. Back in 1970, *Rest in Peace, Uncle Fred* had contained a full-blooded attack on the organised church and I received a letter from a woman in Bournemouth saying she was deeply offended but she would pray for my soul just the same. It's fair to say that things have gone pretty well in the intervening years so maybe there's something in it, unless it only works in Bournemouth.

Even today half the letters people send refer to *Beiderbecke*. One of my favourite correspondents was Molly in Greenock – birthplace of the great Scottish comedian, Chic Murray – who once wrote to say that she loved the music of Fats Waller but needed to know whether this was all right. Would I please give my approval? Which I did, by return of post.

A young couple wrote to say they were exactly like Trevor and Jill in the *Beiderbecke* series. He taught woodwork, she taught English and every so often as an act of homage they'd read aloud from the *Beiderbecke* novels while getting smashed out of their heads on Frascati.

A jeweller in Preston wrote saying he and his wife loved *Beiderbecke* and the next time we were in the area, would we like to come to tea?

But the best of all arrived via the internet connection of a friend in Birmingham. It was from a man in Moline, Illinois, in the United States. He asked about *The Beiderbecke Trilogy* which he'd heard about without being able to track down either the series or the books.

Why was this exciting? Because the correspondent's name was Chris Beiderbecke and I quote: 'Bix Beiderbecke is my great-uncle and I live directly across the Mississippi river from Davenport, Iowa, Bix's hometown.'

If you think about it, this is like Samuel Beckett getting a fax from Godot or Shakespeare a postcard from Hamlet's nephew saying: weather good in Elsinore, wish you were here. But I know which I prefer.

I also picked up, on somebody's grapevine, that Bix was celebrated in his home town by an annual 'Fun Run'. The idea of one of jazz music's most celebrated drunks – in a trade where it has been something of a speciality over the decades – being commemorated by an athletic event, simply confirms my long-held guiding principle. It doesn't matter what you invent, the dedicated madness of the so-called real world will overtake you and leave your imaginary universe gasping in its wake.

As for Bix, I remain forever in his debt. Like Miles Davis, he took his pain and made it beautiful. His music was the true Birth of the Cool. Alan Barnes and I would write a song for him, but Dave Frishberg got there first. His 'Dear Bix', which I use as the title of this chapter, is a gem of a tribute: total perfection.

One day in the mid-nineties the telephone rang. On the line was Jim Simpson, Midlands-based jazz impresario, fixer and begetter of good things musical.

'Alan, how do you feel about doing a one-night stand at Ronnie Scott's in Birmingham, with Kenny Baker? It would be part of the Birmingham Readers' and Writers' Festival.'

'Great. You're on.'

We agreed a date.

Next day the telephone rang again. On the line was Kenny.

'This gig we're doing in Birmingham. . . what's it about?'

'You'll be there with the guys and you'll play some tunes. You know lots of tunes, don't you?'

'But what will *you* be doing?'

'I'm not quite sure. I'll probably write some stories. And on the night I'll tell them. I'll tell a story, you'll play a tune. And then more of the same.'

'OK. See you in Birmingham.'

It was the beginning of our occasional road show, *Beiderbecke and All That Jazz*. For me, it was a dream ticket into a fantasy life of travelling with a band without having

KENNY   A.

gone to the time and trouble of learning to play an instrument: of hanging out with heroes like Roy Williams, Brian Dee and Alan Barnes and listening to their tall tales; and discovering the massive bonus that they hadn't heard my tall tales from the worlds of television and theatre.

The stories I told onstage were much like this book: an extended yarn about adventures with music: about falling in love with bands like Big Bill Campbell's; about failing to tune a zither, fixing a guitar with a missing note, and graduating from being a Flying Fletcher to the one and only Great Prudhoe. Kenny always referred to my stories as 'Alan's patter' which might have struck some of our more esoteric playwrights as vaguely patronising, until you realise that this man had shared top billing in variety theatres with

Morecambe and Wise. If he was ready to bracket me with Eric and Ernie, the top patterers of our time, that was fine by me.

The word I will always associate with Kenny is joy – and most of all the sheer joy he took in making music and in sharing it. Jazz musicians, like playwrights, tend to fall into two categories: the artists, who work mainly for their own benefit, and the entertainers, who work for the benefit of the audience. Kenny – like Armstrong and Ellington – was an artist who saw himself as an entertainer. There was no false pride about the man.

His energy, even in his mid- to late-seventies, was boundless and infectious. Like Tigger, he never stopped bouncing, and he rarely stopped talking. While telling my stories I often heard him chatting away to the other musicians, instantly re-arranging whatever arrangement he'd made for the next number.

The musicians had to be on their toes at all times. One evening we did the show in Hull, at the Spring Street Theatre, scene of so much in the way of financial trauma but now enjoying a mini-boom. Alan Barnes was unavailable – 'I've got a better gig at less money,' he explained – and depping for him was Nigel Hitchcock, a young tenor player and a ferocious exponent of the post-bop tradition.

One of the pieces the band always played was a more or less straight-ahead version of 'Jazz Me Blues'. As Nigel was about to play his solo, Kenny wandered over to him and murmured, gently but firmly: 'Play it like Frankie Trumbauer.' The Spring Street performance also has a unique place in the history of broadcasting. It was recorded by the BBC and later transmitted on Radio 3's *Jazz Notes*. One of the high spots – though, like all high spots, I suppose it depends on your point of view – was a re-creation of my appearance as one of the Forty-Four Flying Fletchers. I did my invisible juggling while Bobby Worth added the spot effects on drums. We were always very disappointed if we didn't get a round of applause, but the Hull audience didn't let us down.

I claim this as the only ever example of invisible juggling being heard on Radio 3.

We were shattered when Kenny died in 1999. We had him marked down as immortal. The mighty Bruce Adams inherited the trumpet chair in the show and that, in its turn, was to lead to many new adventures; but let us now praise Kenny Baker.

I have a bootleg audio-cassette of his last appearance with the *Beiderbecke and All That Jazz* show at Tunbridge Wells. At the end, during our encore – 'The Totally Spontaneous Officially Designated and Well-Honed Encore Blues in F' – I introduce Kenny with the words: 'the only trumpet player banned from playing within a fifty mile radius of Jericho' – whereupon Kenny explodes into his solo like a twenty-year-old: the new kid on the block, fresh from Yorkshire, eager to show London's city slickers and the world beyond how it's done.

He did that for over sixty years. He showed the world how it's done, shared the joy and, above all, he never made the mistake of growing up.

The Motorway Jump

Schlepping around the country with the band gave me a vivid insight into the jazz life of one-night stands in strange-sounding places with faraway names, with accommodation ranging from the luxurious (in Southport, to satisfy the curious) to the more unspeakable brand of B & B, sometimes with the added bonus of a Mrs Vlad running the joint.

We also refined our knowledge of the motorway network of the United Kingdom and it seemed to me that our roads have been largely neglected by the song-writers in this country, unlike America where you can't walk for more than a block in any major city without hitting a song title.

This was my response.

> Take a trip, take a car, take a mac and go forth
> Find the sign saying Hatfield and the North
> Get your kicks
> On the A66
> Be like Jacky Horner
> Sitting at Scotch Corner
> Eating your pie and peas
> Leave the straight and narrow
> Head across to Barrow
> Live yourself a life of ease
> Listen out to the message I'm singing to you
> If you want to be handy for Keswick and Crewe
> Get your kicks
> On the A66

Maybe you want to drive where the highway is wide
And it isn't so easy for people to hide
Seems like you
Need the M62
There's a swinging function
At spaghetti junction
The disco leaves you deaf
You'll find the silence golden
On the road to Oldham
Have a bacon butty at the Little Chef
It's a free world out there, you have to decide
The magic direction that you want to ride
Up to you
On the M62

Do I see one or two of you down in the mouth?
Do you think life is sweeter way down in the South?
Jump and jive
To the M25
Hear the sirens blaring
Ambulances haring
An incident at Exit 10
Eventually clears up
Everybody cheers up
Foot hard on the pedal and begin again
Close your eyes to the trucker who's just shed his load
And the maniac four-wheelers filling the road
Stay alive
On the M25

They say all roads lead to Rome
But me, I'm gonna stay home
You can stick
The A66
You can screw
The M62
I'll survive
Without the M25
Oh yeah!

ON THE ROAD WITH THE BAND

A Belgian stand-up comedian called Joris once said to me:
'Imagine – if the Italian artists of the Renaissance hadn't
invented the rules of perspective, we wouldn't be able to
drive along motorways.'

6.

Doggin' Around

It should be clear by now that I've never had anything resembling a career plan. Much of what I've written has been an unplanned collision of unrelated incidents. A couple of these took place sometime in the mid-eighties.

The first was a letter from an old friend, the actor Jack Shepherd. Jack had arrived as a student in Newcastle just as I was leaving. We may well have passed each other in the Central Station, him bright with wide-eyed anticipation of a golden future, me with a suitcase full of failed examinations and old regrets. Had he been a year older and therefore a year earlier in arriving he could well have become a Flying Fletcher, in which case the course of history could have been transformed. It's possible he wouldn't have spoken to me again and therefore wouldn't have been writing me letters in the mid-eighties.

But he did. The letter told me that he'd been in an episode of a Granada television series called *Bulman*, in which he played a Russian jazz musician who had defected to the West. The guy was a tenor player and – this was the crucial bit – Jack had done all his own playing and, by way of proof, he sent me a tape of the music. The message was simple: if I ever fancied writing a nice part for a tenor player, Jack was my man. The character didn't have to be a Russian. He could be from anywhere in the world, or from any galaxy not yet discovered or explored, as long as he played tenor.

The second incident was a conversation with television producer, Jonathan Powell, who had overseen my dramatisation of Anthony Trollope's *The Warden* and *Barchester Towers* into what became *Barchester Chronicles*. Jonathan was zooming through the ranks, on his way to becoming Controller of BBC1, and he had a proposition.

'Look, we don't have to go on proving that the BBC can do classic serials. I think we should be doing more contemporary work. Television novels set in the present day. Write the book and write the series.'

'Does it matter in which order?

'You're the writer. You decide.'

It was an intoxicating offer though writers do tend to intoxicate easily. I slapped the two unrelated incidents together and started work. The central character would be a tenor player looking remarkably like Jack Shepherd. I fed a few current obsessions into the mix and then – as Gus never quite said in *Drop the Dead Donkey* – I ran them through the blender to see what congealed.

The obsessions included father-daughter relationships, Jewishness and Johnny Hodges.

The mere fact that I mention it means that I have a good relationship with my daughter, and not the sort that needs acres of pyscho-babble. What we share is an attachment to truth. About a dozen years ago she wrote a tough and well-received radio play. Since then she's shown little inclination to write any more and instead has become a good and highly-respected actors' agent in the North of England. What she said was:

'I don't think I'll write any more plays for a while, Dad. Do you mind? I might start again after you're dead.'

'Deal.'

Which says as much as anyone needs to know.

Around the same time that the Jack Shepherd/Jonathan Powell axis was at work I married for the second time. My wife, Shirley, is Jewish, and I found myself warmly embraced by a whole new extended family, and when a Jewish family embraces you – trust me – you stay embraced. Would I lie about such a thing?

The plot – to the extent that my work ever has much of a plot – quickly fell into place. Daughter is conceived as a result of a brief but passionate affair between two students at Leeds University. The parents forbid marriage because the father is Jewish. Mum marries someone else and then, twenty-five years later, is killed in a car crash.

Daughter, now living a tranquil life in York with a young architect, sorts through her papers and discovers Dad isn't her biological father. She tracks down her real father, who's running a jazz club in London. This is where Johnny Hodges came into the equation. I'd just bought a Duke Ellington album (I was down to about two hundred) and one of the tracks was a Hodges version of 'On Green Dolphin Street' – totally beguiling but did he ever record anything that wasn't? It made total sense from my point of view. The jazz club would be called Green Dolphin Street. The tune would be the clue to the mystery, the magical theme that haunted the series.

Everything was in place. All I had to do was start writing. Then I got the phone call. Jonathan Powell would like me to come in for a chat.

'How's it all going?'

'It's going fine.'

I told him about Jack Shepherd, Jewish families and Johnny Hodges.

'Good. But would you mind stopping for a while?'

'Why?'

'We'd like you to dramatise *Fortunes of War.*'

I had no idea what he was talking about. He spotted my blank stare. They're never hard to spot.

'Six novels by Olivia Manning. According to the critics the best novels written about the Second World War.'

'I remember the war. I was in an air-raid shelter in Hull.'

'The novels are set in the Balkans and Egypt.'

The stare went a little less blank. The eyes probably lit up though I can't be sure.

'Could. . . research trips come into this?'

'I'm sure we can arrange something.'

I spent the next year turning sixteen hundred pages of paperback into a seven episode series starring Kenneth Branagh, Emma Thompson and Ronald Pickup, punctuated by a jolly research trip to Athens and a scary one to Ceausescu's Bucharest.

Our producer was a legendary woman called Betty Willingale who loves writing and writers and often knows more about them than they do themselves. We were having supper when on location in Zagreb (which was pretending to be Bucharest) and I told her about my Great Novel.

'It's called *On Green Dolphin Street.*'

'It's been used,' said Betty.

'What!!!???'

I spluttered into my slivovitz while Betty explained that *Green Dolphin Street* was a novel written by Elizabeth

Goudge that she'd read years ago. As soon as I returned home I flew to my *Halliwell* and discovered that the book had been filmed in 1947, starring Lana Turner, Van Heflin and Edmund Gwenn. The strapline apparently ran: 'A fiery girl dares the dangers of the sea and a strange land – fighting for the love of a bold adventurer!'

Pauline Kael of the *New Yorker*, the greatest film critic of our time, wrote of the film: 'The actors in this stupefyingly flimsy epic seem to be in competition for the booby prizes.' But Bronislaw Kaper had written the music and given the jazz world a memorable theme so it wasn't all bad news.

There seemed little chance that the two projects would ever be confused. I never write about bold adventurers and, therefore, there's never been any need to write about fiery girls fighting for their love. My adventurers, such as they are, tend to be shy, slippered and apologetic, and if they have adventures it's usually by mistake.

In addition, there is no copyright on titles. You may call your play *Twelfth Night*, *Hedda Gabler* or *The Cherry Orchard*, and nobody has any legal right to stop you. A marvellously eccentric English writer called J. L. Carr wrote a lovely novel called *A Month in the Country* and when the publishers reminded him it had already been used he commented: 'Good enough for Ivan Turgenev, good enough for me.'

On the other hand, getting cute with titles can have long-term consequences. In 1966 I was commissioned to write three episodes for *Z Cars* at a time when the BBC was keen to keep me out of the grasp of those wicked commercial people in ITV. In later years it would be known as a golden handcuffs deal though back then gold wasn't really involved: just a few coppers.

For the purposes of the contract there had to be three episode titles but at the signature stage I had no idea what any of them was to be about. But without titles it seemed the sky would fall on the BBC contracts department, so I suggested, purely to fill the spaces: *Hamlet, Son of Hamlet* and *Carry on Hamlet*.

Years later my agent would have phone calls from the BBC saying things like: 'We have a cheque for three pounds for a repeat showing in Hong Kong of a *Z Cars* episode called *Carry on Hamlet*. Can you explain this phenomenon?'

I decided to avoid all that, by using a totally different piece of music, thereby changing the title of the book and what eventually became, not a series, but a one-off film starring Jack Shepherd. Naturally.

The piece I chose was 'Misterioso'.

In the story our man is called Paul Webster. It's a triple homage. Paul after Paul Gonsalves, Webster after Ben Webster and Paul Webster was a great trumpet player with the Jimmy Lunceford band.

When his long-lost daughter, Rachel, tracks him down to his club in London, he talks about 'Misterioso'.

'It's a piece of music. A blues, naturally, like all my best friends. Written by Thelonious Monk. Piano player, full name – Thelonious Sphere Monk. If you're a musician, you'll understand me when I say it's a blues built around walking sixths.

If you're not a musician, let me offer my congratulations and tell you "Misterioso" is a tune that haunts you. Always beyond reach. Just around the corner. A sweet promise and the echo of a sad dream.'

'What a load of pretentious crap,' is the reaction of both mother and daughter, at the key stages in their relationship with Paul.

Where *Misterioso* differed from, say, the *Beiderbecke* series, was that not only was the music a character but so were the musicians. It was my first attempt to depict, on the page and on the screen, something of the everyday life of jazz musicians, though perhaps that should be the everynight life, since it's essentially an occupation that flourishes after dark. I'd fallen in love with bands as a kid sitting in the stalls of the Palace and the Tivoli in Hull, watching Harry Roy and Big Bill Campbell, and now I was able to live out my fantasies in the only way I knew – by writing about them.

The book was published in 1987 and was reviewed extensively in one newspaper, one monthly magazine and much of the jazz press. Most of the latter assumed that I had modelled Paul Webster directly on Ronnie Scott. I knew, obviously, that Ronnie was a tenor player who ran a jazz club, and was vaguely aware that he was Jewish – hence his joke about the guy who mixed chopped liver with cannabis and took a trip to Israel. But I didn't know he had a daughter – not exactly long-lost but close enough to make me nervous.

I bit the bullet. I wrote to Ronnie, enclosing a signed copy of the book, with a covering letter saying any resemblances were totally coincidental and assuring him that no tenor players were harmed in the writing of the novel. He replied, promptly and generously, saying he'd enjoyed the book enormously and had no intention of suing.

Fortunately we already had what the politicians call a 'special relationship' with the club. Shirley and I were there one night in 1986 and, browsing in the house magazine, discovered you could hire the club on a Sunday night for a private function.

'What a great place to have a party,' said Shirley. 'What could we do to justify it?'

THE SECRET OF A HAPPY MARRIAGE

'Will you marry me?' I said.

And that's what happened. We married at Camden Registry Office on Saturday September 27th 1986 and had the party at Ronnie's the following evening. An old friend from the North, Bernie Cash, led the band on bass and, in the interests of completeness, the rest of them were Stan Robinson (tenor), Ray Manderson (trumpet), Dave Cliff (guitar) and Mark Taylor (drums). Shirley and I led the dancing to 'Lester Leaps In'.

What a swell party it was. As one of our guests said: 'It was wonderful. Even the waiters and waitresses were pissed.'

My best man, Tom Courtenay, made a splendid speech and was gracious enough to tell everyone of the record I'd set up in school: the youngest kid to play for the second eleven at football without ever making the first. The documentary director, John Jeremy, brought the American singer, Cynthia McPherson, over from Paris as his wedding present and she sang 'My Funny Valentine' for us. All the proceedings were given permanent form on probably the most impenetrable video in the history of home movies. John Worth, composer of many a hit song for Adam Faith in his heyday, used Vince Hill's camera. On the face of it, this is a somewhat unlikely friendship, but I had collaborated with John and Vince on a stage musical called *Zodiac* and, despite a couple of adventurous amateur productions, twenty years on we are still waiting for it to go to the West End and Broadway and make us into millionaires.

Any professional, and most good amateurs, will tell you that a pre-requisite of photography is light. Unfortunately Ronnie's is more famous for darkness, with the result that when John looked through the viewfinder, about the only thing he could see was the wedding cake. Nevertheless, the video *Al and Shirl at Ronnie Scott's* has a place of honour on our special shelves.

The relationship with Ronnie and the club was further strengthened in 1989. The BBC celebrated the club's thirtieth anniversary with a documentary and I was interviewed as part of the programme. I wore a Lester Young hat given to me by one of our kids and, thus garbed, read an extract from *Misterioso* and talked about the special atmosphere of the place. I said: 'There's only thing that could spoil it. A single shaft of sunlight.'

A couple of weeks later we were in the club and Ronnie displayed, by his standards, an enormous outpouring of emotion.

'Hey, that was really nice what you said.'

Later a bottle of champagne arrived at our table with the message: there'll be another one in thirty years time. Then, a few days later, I received a gold membership card in the post, entitling us to free admission for life. If that isn't a special relationship, I don't know what is; and there was much more as the years passed by.

I think it was Sammy Cahn who, when asked 'How do your songs begin?' replied, 'With a telephone call.' The same applies to most of my plays.

Norman McCandlish, a fine television producer who did years of wonderful work for BBC Scotland – also an authority on single malts, rugby union and curling – called:

'I've been reading *Misterioso*. Has anyone acquired the television rights?'

'Not that I'm aware of.'

'May I have them please?'

'Of course. Unless I have to reset the whole thing in Glasgow or Auchtermuchty.'

'Don't be silly. Remember who you're talking to.'

'Sorry, Norman.'

The only conditions – neither of them onerous – were that Jack Shepherd should play the lead and Frank Ricotti should be in charge of the music.

It's axiomatic that if you get the casting right in drama, most other things will follow. The minute James Bolam and Barbara Flynn picked up the Beiderbecke scripts we were in business. With *Misterioso*, the approach was a mixture of tough professionalism and, in the case of Rachel, sheer chance. We saw a picture in the paper of Suzan Sylvester, who was appearing with the Royal Shakespeare Company.

'Look at that!' I said. 'She's a dead ringer!'

Meaning there was an astonishing likeness to my daughter. We arranged for them to come round for supper. We sat them side by side and, aside from the fact they were both dark and beautiful, there was no resemblance whatsoever;

but Suzan had that special quality of appearing to hear music in her head and she was subsequently cast to play Rachel. This, incidentally, is the kind of story likely to drive actors into despair and an immediate career change.

Suzan didn't have to play anything. Most of the time she was there to listen, the truest test of any actor: all the good ones are great listeners.

Then we moved on to the musician characters. The central challenge of putting musicians on screen is making them look as if they are really playing. The obvious answer is to cast people who can really play – which is pretty much where we came in, with Jack Shepherd.

There were two main characters where this was a vital element: Mike Daley, a gentle guy and gentle piano player in the Bill Evans/Keith Jarrett tradition and Ray Gardner, a ferocious visiting American trumpet player given to insulting everybody within reach. Gardner was inspired by the tales I'd heard of Ruby Braff who once, according to legend, had yelled at George Wein when they were onstage at Newport:

'Just play the changes, George. Stop trying to express yourself.'

Bill Bryden, a brilliant theatre director who had become Head of Drama for BBC Scotland, and an even greater expert on single malt than Norman McCandlish, was keen to cast the man himself.

'I'll tell him to his face. "Ruby, we're told you're an evil bastard. Well, the character's an evil bastard and it takes one to play one. Welcome aboard. What are you drinking?"'

In the end, calmer counsels prevailed. Mike Daley was played by Paul Stacey, a wonderful jazz guitarist and key member of the early Tommy Smith bands, and totally at ease with a piano keyboard. And as Ray Gardner we cast

Bill Berry, the American cornet/trumpet player, who played like an angel and behaved like one too. To make my life complete, he was an ex-Ellingtonian.

He was infinitely patient and would answer my anorak questions with great warmth and generosity of spirit.

Some examples:

'Why do you play cornet instead of trumpet?'

'It isn't as heavy.'

'Who was your favourite Ellington trumpet player?'

'Harold Shorty Baker.'

'Why?'

'Because he would play the tune beautifully.'

He revered the Duke, not least for his enlightened racial attitudes. Bill was one of the few white musicians to play in the band and whenever Ellington was questioned about this he would reply: 'I've always run an integrated band. I only employ musicians.'

Bill also had a treasure-chest of jazz anecdotes of the kind that illuminate the wee small hours. My favourite – which I later appropriated and used in the *Beiderbecke* road show, though always credited to Bill – was about the West Coast trumpet player, Jack Sheldon. Sheldon was out on the streets during the riots in Los Angeles and reprimanded a woman who was looting from a shop window with the words:

'Lady, you simply cannot loot those shoes with that handbag.'

The novel of *Misterioso* is long out of print and the film hasn't been seen in years, but it does seem to linger in some people's memories. Not so long ago I had a letter from a young man in the Home Counties. His dad had a big birthday coming up and what he would like most of all was a video of *Misterioso*. Could we help? What clinched it was his last line.

'As proof of my honesty and integrity, I am a great fan of the 1940 Ellington band – the one with Ben Webster and Jimmy Blanton.'

I bet Harold Pinter and Tom Stoppard don't get letters like that.

Writing original film scripts is much like backing the out-sider in a field of twenty-five. Writing original film scripts about jazz is much the same, except your horse did a milk round before coming to the course. I'm told by people who know such things that no jazz movie has ever made money. These apparently include the best three ever made which, in my order of preference, are *Sven Klang's Combo*, *Round Midnight* and *Bird*, though Woody Allen deserves more credit than he's ever likely to get for the impeccable musical taste he's demonstrated throughout his movie career.

The experts go on to tell us that the only film in this genre to show a profit was *The Glenn Miller Story* and we can all draw our own conclusions from that information. Cast James Stewart as Charlie Parker and you solve all your problems?

In that context any producer who encourages a screen-writer to contemplate a jazz movie should be given the BAFTA award for Recklessness. Such a man was Leslie Linder, an independent producer long before it was fash-ionable. He approached me sometime in the mid-eighties with a couple of questions. The first question was:

Did I know that Jack Lemmon was a fine piano player and a jazz fan?

No I didn't.

The second question was: didn't I think it time somebody wrote a decent screen role for Cleo Laine?

Yes I did.

In retrospect, I'm not even sure Cleo knew what was going on, and I must ask her. Either way it was an offer I couldn't refuse and I slipped into gear with wary enthusiasm, knowing what the experts said about jazz movies.

As usual my plot was slender like gossamer. An American jazz pianist plays a tour of Northern venues but – because on a previous tour he has left a trail of betrayed women, bookmakers and agents of the law – he is sent out with a minder, whose job is to keep him out of trouble. The minder is a former jazz singer who quit the business because of her bad experiences with a piano player. At the end, she sings again. In Hollywood they'd call it a Sleeping Beauty plot. Overall, it matched my present agent's description of my narrative approach: two people who are old enough to know better go on the road and get up to mischief. I adorned the story with some lovely music and affectionate gags about the Deep North, and called it *Doggin' Around*. The piano player was called Joe Warren and all the principal characters were named after members of the Count Basie band.

I delivered the screenplay, Leslie liked it very much, it did the rounds of the money people, ten years passed by and nothing happened. The rights expired and I'd forgotten about it until Otto Plaschkes, another independent producer, said he'd like to work with me and was there anything on the shelf I'd like him to look at? By this time we were into the nineties, every third person in north London was an independent producer, but Otto was one of the 0.0000001 per cent who could actually do the job, and had a track record for evidence. I gave him *Doggin' Around* to read and he loved it.

Meanwhile, in another part of the forest – to be precise, in Shepherds Bush – the fates were working in our favour. The BBC had hired Margaret Matheson, yet another independent producer who could actually do it, to work in-house for a while and oversee a series of films under the banner title of *Screen One*. Everything was going smoothly until she discovered, at quite a late stage, that whereas she thought she was producing six films, the BBC thought she was producing eight.

Fortunately, Margaret is a very bright and resourceful woman. In a previous professional incarnation, she'd been head of production for one of the main outfits in town that found the money for this kind of exercise. She remembered a couple of screenplays she'd turned down (for perfectly proper reasons at the time) and made some calls. They were still available. One of them was Victoria Wood's *Pat and Margaret*. The other was *Doggin' Around*.

The deal that the BBC presented to Otto Plaschkes on a Friday, was: 'Get us a big American star by Monday and we'll make the film.'

I don't know the precise mechanics of the operation but somehow copies of the screenplay found their way to Elliott Gould and George Segal in L.A. over the week-end. In my mind I see them being delivered by a gang of black leather-clad motor-cyclists led by Marlon Brando but I could be wrong. On the Sunday evening Otto telephoned me:

'Elliott Gould and George Segal both love the script.'

'Oh. What happens next?'

'We have to decide which one to cast.'

'Can't we do two versions?'

'No.'

'Oh.'

'You're the writer. You have to decide.'

They're both terrific, but if ever there was an actor who *looks* like an archetypal jazz musician, it's Elliott Gould. It's an after-hours face that has heard the blues at midnight.

Elliott became a key member of a dream team and made a good job of looking as if he was playing the piano, though the notes were supplied by Dave Hartley. His minder was played by Geraldine James, who mimed to the singing voice of Norma Winstone. Ewan McGregor played a brash young bass player, with Alun Armstrong as an archetypal Northern jazz fan who knew who played what and where at every gig in the last thirty years. Frank Ricotti was in charge of the music and the film was directed by the gentle and talented Desmond Davis.

Unusually, we had a whole week of rehearsal before we started shooting and I turned up on Day One a little nervously. I knew Elliott had done much of his finest work with the great Robert Altman, who encourages his actors to improvise freely and generally kick the dialogue around the place. To my surprise and delight, Elliott was determined to be word perfect though he did take me aside at an early stage for an earnest consultation.

'Alan. I have a problem with this line.'

He showed me the line in the script.

'You see, he used the word "isn't".'

'Yes, Elliott. It's short for "is not" – that's why there's an inverted comma, to show something's been left out.'

'Sure, I know what "isn't" means. But see, I come from Brooklyn, and I really do think I should say "ain't". But only if it's all right with you.'

'Elliott, in all matters pertaining to Brooklyn, you are a leading authority. Feel free to change it, or anything else for that matter.'

'No, that's the only one.'

He corrected the script and that was the only thing we changed.

The least relevant character in the film is a walk-on part described in the screenplay as 'Man in pork-pie hat'. He is seen entering Ronnie Scott's at the opening of the film and later glimpsed sleeping off a hangover in the lobby of the club the next morning.

Desmond Davis and Otto Plaschkes decided, unilaterally, that I should play the part. In the trade it's called doing a Hitchcock. With the impenetrable logic that goes with film-making the opening shot of the movie – Man in pork-pie hat arrives at Ronnie's in pouring rain – was the final sequence to be shot. That's how it happened that I found myself on a baking hot Sunday night in Soho, walking along Frith Street in my best suit, pork-pie hat and carrying an umbrella while the fire brigade sprayed water on me from a great height. A sizeable crowd gathered to watch though their interest diminished once they realised I wasn't anybody they'd heard of but just some anonymous idiot walking along a street.

It was important that I get it right as quickly as possible because most of the cast and crew were gathering for the end-of-shoot party in a bar around the corner. In the midst of the crowd Shirley found Elliott sitting in a doorway across the street. He was wearing tee-shirt and shorts, was bearded and amiably grizzled.

'Elliott,' she said. 'If you sit there like that, people are likely to give you money.'

'Shirley, they already have.'

Doggin' Around was also noteworthy because it contained Ronnie Scott's only acting performance. He played the part of a tenor player and jazz club proprietor called Ronnie Scott.

In the course of this he has to take a crucial telephone call. It went something like this:

'Yes, speaking. (*listens then:*) He's dead? (*listens then:*) Is it serious? (*listens then:*) Does this mean he can't do the tour? (*listens then:*) So what's the bad news? (*he listens and then writes the name "Joe Warren" on a pad.*) Yes, that is bad news.'

At the time Ronnie told a national newspaper he'd only accepted the part on condition he didn't have to take his clothes off unless, he added, it was integral to the drama.

When Ronnie died, it was suggested that I might write a book about the man and the club. It didn't come to anything but, to this day, I'm fascinated by the unique place it holds in the nation's culture – and I don't apologise for using the word. It's a precise definition.

Apart from the Theatre Royal, Stratford East, Ronnie's is the only place in London where we can walk past the queues and be greeted with hugs and insults, simultaneously, by the front-of-house staff. I once turned up wearing a new pair of sneakers, bought – actually at a very reasonable price – in France. They sat me down, removed the shoes and passed them round for closer inspection.

'Hey, man, we love the shoes. Where did you get them?'

'Paris. Where else does one buy shoes?'

Ronnie was the ultimate night person and the club, by definition, exists for night people. To be sure, that's a romantic concept, freely available only to the self-employed, except at weekends when people with proper jobs may become associate members. And there's an element of self-delusion involved. Some of us actually *like* to look like 'something a stone crawled out from over' – to quote Dick Vosburgh.

By definition, musicians are night people and most creative people lean in that direction. Art is made in our dreams. Where else can it happen? Increasingly I tend to assess people according to St Matthew's Gospel: by their musical tastes and nocturnal habits ye shall know them.

All that being so (and because some of it is self-evident bollocks) Ronnie was an icon and a role model. He raised self-deprecation to the level of an art form. Of his quintet he would say: 'Five musicians who have brought a great deal of pleasure to very few people.' Of his bass player: 'I've played with a lot of bass players in my time and he's one of them.' Of his club: 'You should have been here last week. *Somebody* should have been here last week. We had the bouncers chucking them *in*.'

This attitude spread sideways throughout his team. Some years ago *Private Eye* ran an item claiming the club had become tawdry and down-at-heel. Pete King, club manager and Ronnie's formidable partner wrote in reply: 'We haven't become tawdry and down-at-heel. We've *always* been tawdry and down-at-heel.'

There's also a tale on record about a member of the front-of-house staff, under siege during one of George Melly's Christmas seasons. A customer turned up, demanding entrance with the words: 'But I'm a close personal friend of Mr Melly's,' and was told: 'What do you want me to do? Jump up in the fucking air?'

There are words to describe the attitude: hip and cool are a couple but strictly inadequate because words of that sort have a brief shelf-life. The American pianist, Dave Frishberg, wrote a song called 'I'm Hip' which parodies changing dimensions of cool and contains the line:

'When it was hip to be hep I was hep.'

Quite so. And recently I read that the young rock musicians now prove they're truly alternative and rebellious by hoovering their hotel rooms instead of trashing them. Tomorrow it will be something different. Chances are they'll buy a controlling interest in the hotel.

Jazz clubs, and Ronnie's in particular, are about nightness: the otherness, the subterraneanness, the Left Bankness, the all-the-things-your-parents-warned-you-against-ness. They celebrate a form of music which is, in my judgement, the major creative contribution made by the human race to the twentieth century. I say this because it is democratic – anyone who can play can join in the music – and because it celebrates the human spirit while not denying the pain. Miles Davis does all that in one note. The whole of the rock/pop so-called revolution is an offspring of jazz. The great black rhythm-and-blues singers begat Bill Haley and Elvis Presley who, in turn, begat the Beatles, who took the form but revolutionised the content with lovely tales of Penny Lane and meter maids. But the main theme of 'Can't Buy Me Love' is a twelve bar blues.

Even so, jazz tends to be hurled by sub-editors into a pigeon-hole marked FOR OLD FARTS ONLY, despite the fact there are more young musicians playing the music – and playing it better – than at any time in our history. There are racial and ethnic dimensions to this, allied to a profound historical change that happened in society, unnoticed by most people apart from the criminal records office, in the 1980s.

The change was this. When robberies took place at music shops, the thieves began to steal saxophones instead of guitars. It is my belief that this reflected a realisation that the three guitars and a drummer form that comprised the Beatles and most of the pop/rock music that followed had run its course. There is a limit to the sounds you can make with guitars. There is no limit to the range of sounds you can produce with a greater variety of instruments. The thieves knew this, presumably because they'd done their market research.

Soon after Ronnie died I took a phone call from a friend in Canada, a guy called Tom who runs workshops for film makers. When he and his wife had visited London the previous year they had a request. Would we take them to Ronnie's? And we did.

On the phone Tom said: 'That was the only time we went to the club but we were shattered to hear of Ronnie's death. We cried and thought of you.'

I once had a conversation with my youngest son, who's an engineer working in computers. I was moaning about the then preponderance of television series set in the Second World War.

'I don't understand it,' I said.

'Oh, it's simple, Dad,' he replied. 'We've reached that moment in time when memory becomes history.'

'Obviously,' I said, wondering what it is in engineering that produces such insight.

Later I arrived at the tentative conclusion that all human experience goes through the same stages: memory becomes history and history becomes legend. That's why politicians like to grab hold of the history, publish their memoirs and try (generally in vain) to make sure of their place in the legend.

Ronnie and the club that bears his name made it to legendary status, but they did it the cool way – without trying.

I'm Still Playing Cherokee

One of the many famous stories about Ronnie's concerns the night of the first moon landings: the giant step for all mankind gig. Zoot Sims was playing at the club that week. He was among those watching in the office backstage and commented: 'Imagine. We've got men on the moon and I'm still playing fucking "Cherokee".'

This song is a tribute to Zoot Sims, Ronnie Scott, and tenor players the world over who never did anything more lethal than play 'Cherokee'.

> There are people on the moon
> And very very soon
> They'll be running Sergeant Bilko on a Sunday afternoon
> And me?
> I'm still playing Cherokee
> We're running out of snow
> And the ice-caps are aglow
> If you want to buy a paper then you'd better learn to row
> But me?
> I'm still playing Cherokee
>
> Got to face it
> The earth
> Is facing
> A dearth
> Of all the stuff we need to keep us going
> Got to say it
> The world
> Is coming
> Unfurled
> You must have noticed grandpa gently glowing

We're destroying the planet
We're down to the last gannet
And we're heading for oblivion says my second cousin Janet
But me
I'm still playing Cherokee
The skies are looking leaden
The seas begin to deaden
The Guardian editorial says we're in for Armageddon
Don't blame me
I was only playing Cherokee

Birds no longer sing
Who has done this thing?
Not me
I'm still playing Cherokee

7.

The Joint is Jumping

When asked to define my nationality I've developed a stock line: 'Geordie by birth, Yorkshire by upbringing and now a metropolitan sophisticate.' It generally gets a cheap laugh, which is the main object of the exercise, and possibly of my entire existence.

Shirley and I moved to London in 1984 to start a new chapter in both our lives and, a couple of years later, a new marriage. Georges Simenon, the man who gave Inspector Maigret to the world, once defined his writing method as placing his characters in a close relationship and then testing it to destruction. Shirley discovered that a very good way of doing this is to move in with someone who is trying to set lyrics to jazz improvisations – the form known as vocalese, made into a minor art form by Eddie Jefferson and by Lambert, Hendricks and Ross. It was yet another example of ending up doing something without meaning to. It wasn't my fault. It never is.

Bernie Cash was a fine bass player who, in the 1980s, was living in Bridlington in Yorkshire. He was also a great talker. We once asked him how he'd ended up in Bridlington and the answer went on for an hour or more, involved National Service in the RAF, playing trumpet with Harry Gold and his Pieces of Eight, meeting Dorothy Dandridge at an Oxbridge May Ball and being sacked by Bruce Turner; but we never found out how he'd ended up in Bridlington.

His many activities included playing in symphony orchestras, running a youth big band in Hull and the East Riding, forming a rhythm section with Mark Taylor and Dave Cliff to back Bob Wilber and Kenny Davern when they toured the UK with Soprano Summit, and organising gigs around the city which, on a good night, attracted the usual 172 suspects, most of whom we knew by name. In his spare time, and to avoid boredom, Bernie had done a music doctorate at Hull University, with a written thesis on the solos of Lester Young. This gave him an idea. Such men are dangerous. Try to be out when they call.

Bernie's idea was to write a chamber opera about Lester, and, of course, Billie Holiday, using the solos as the base for the music. Would I do the words? Or, since it was an opera, would I write the libretto?

I had recently written a film about George Orwell and one of the great man's thoughts was wedged in my head and has remained there ever since. He once said: 'It's a pretty safe bet about anything that as long as there's no money in it, it's probably all right.' Bernie's proposition fitted the bill perfectly. The show would play for one week at Spring Street in Hull and possibly a week at the Battersea Arts Centre. Who could refuse such an offer?

Shirley and I had moved on a temporary basis into a rented flat not far from Kings Cross and for the first two weeks of our co-habitation, the only sounds to emerge from my study were those of Lester's solo on 'Lady Be Good', takes one and two, from the 1938 sessions. Shirley didn't even get to hear the tune: only the two solos over and over and over again. And then some more.

The words that eventually emerged went something like this:

> The name's Pres
> They call me Lester Young on Sunday that's all
> I played sweet tenor sax
> As cool and relaxed
> And pretty as pearls
> Listen to the notes playing
> And hear what they're saying
> The joint is jumping
> It's really something to shout about
> Like cascading fountains
> Parading down mountains in summertime days
> I come from New Orleans
> Just like Buddy Bolden and those other guys
> And it's nobody's big surprise
> There is jazz behind my eyes
> Swing high – swing high in the sky
> I am telling you why
> This swinging horn
> Was born to be played by The President!

And that was just the first stanza. It took me a fortnight to write it. Applying time-and-motion studies of the sort John Birt later used to wreck the BBC, it was the same amount of time I would have devoted to:

> One episode of *Barchester Chronicles*.
> Two episodes of *Oh No It's Selwyn Froggitt!*
> Two-thirds of an episode of *Fortunes of War*.

This confirms all the self-evident truths you need to know about jazz. It will never be cost-effective and nothing related to the music ever makes sense.

What came out of all this effort was the sort of show your best friends tell you was 'really interesting'. Alan Cooke played Lester and Carol Kenyon, formerly a singer with NYJO, played Billie. John Jeremy produced a *South Bank Show* about the making of the piece and Melvyn Bragg came round to the flat to interview me, at which point I recreated the making of the 'Lady Be Good' lyrics and Shirley, showing infinite patience and total understanding of the creative process, smiled and brought us coffee.

During the making of the documentary we also talked to Slim Gaillard about Lester and he produced the following gem: 'Lester played real quiet – like a rat walking on silk.'

Pres (or *Prez* – we never quite made up our minds about the spelling) played for a week in Hull and a week in Battersea, with Stan Robinson, Ray Manderson, Dave Cliff, Mark Taylor and Bernie – later to be our wedding band at Ronnie's – plus Nick Weldon, son of Fay, on piano. 'How's your Mum?' became our regular greeting.

Yet again we got mixed reviews. The Hull *Daily Mail* thought it was a bit short: never mind the quality, feel the width, etc, though, as the initial performance only lasted about half-an-hour, there was some justice in the verdict.

Before we moved to downtown Battersea, Bernie expanded some of the instrumental passages. Dave Gelly wrote a generous review in one of the posh Sundays (I remember these things, Dave) and somebody else wrote an ungenerous piece in one of the others. They were probably both right.

The happy sequel is that domestically our relationship survived and prospered, though I haven't rushed to write any more vocalese.

The sad sequel is that Bernie died of a heart attack while out jogging in Germany, where he was on tour with the LSO. At the funeral Stan Robinson played Lester's version of 'Lady Be Good', accompanied by Dave Cliff and Peter Ind on bass.

Nat Shapiro has an honoured place in the history of our music. Born in New York, he became a writer and record producer, responsible for countless albums, including many by Miles Davis. With Nat Hentoff he co-edited one of the classic books on jazz, *Hear Me Talkin' to Ya*, probably the first anthology to present the musicians themselves – from Louis Armstrong, Duke Ellington and Fletcher Henderson to Stan Kenton and Dave Brubeck – talking about what they did, how they did it and why.

When he died in 1983, Nat left outline notes for a stage musical called *Rent Party*, about a Harlem rent party of the 1940s. It had been one of his ambitions to mount such a show on or off Broadway.

In one of those bizarre coincidences that sometimes make the world a jollier place, Nat's wife, Vera, is a longtime family friend of Philip Hedley, for thirty years the artistic director of the Theatre Royal, Stratford East. She showed Nat's notes to Philip.

Philip said: 'I know just the man to write this.'

On the face of it, the idea of a native Geordie, reared in Yorkshire, living in happy exile in north London, writing a musical about Harlem in the 1940s for a theatre in the East End of London, seems like one of the nuttier notions of the twentieth century. That is what made Philip one of the top men in British theatre. His motto, briefly summarised, was: if in doubt, head for the nearest precipice.

But his instincts were, as often, right on the money. Harlem in the 1940s was a poor area with a large black population: so was Stratford East in the 1980s.

Rent Party was part of a larger trend in the theatre of that period, which involved taking a selection of songs and music from the jazz/blues/vaudeville repertoire and presenting them to the audience, gift-wrapped, in a cheerful good-time parcel. *Ain't Misbehavin'*, inspired by Fats Waller, and *Five Guys Named Mo*, from Louis Jordan, were two of the most high-profile examples.

Our show was slightly different in that it had a story, though admittedly it was pretty flimsy. A group of people get together for a party, they are raided by a policeman, somebody pulls the plug on the hooch in the bath-tub, but it turns out the cop isn't really raiding the place, he's come to tell one of the guests – a hustler called Lucky Franklin – that he's won a big cash prize in a marginally illicit lottery running at Tricky Sam's pool-room. So it all ends happily.

As a piece of narrative, it isn't up there with *War and Peace*; but on the other hand, Tolstoy didn't have music first performed by the likes of Bessie Smith, Louis Armstrong, Fats Waller and Duke Ellington. And pursuing the Russian parallels, you will scan the complete works of Anton Chekhov and Maxim Gorki and nowhere will you find an extended twenty-five minute sequence where the characters on stage take turns to sing the blues: from 'St Louis' to 'Trouble in Mind'. Though it does occur to me that a lot of the people in Chekhov and Gorki have the blues; they just don't sing them. It might have helped if they had.

Theatre people are notorious for diving into the deep end of schmaltz when reminiscing about old shows, but the fact remains that working on *Rent Party* was a total joy from beginning to end. Our cast – and let's name them because they deserve it – Clinton Derricks Carroll, Carol Kenyon, Sharon D. Clarke, Melanie Marshall, Robert Coverton, Pearly Gates, Kofi Missah, Louis Emerick and our token white folk, John Turner and Polly Hemingway – were all superb.

And we were blessed to have Colin Purbrook as our musical director. When Clinton, an American from California, came to audition – 'I can sing, dance and act – I'm a triple threat' – Colin caressed the accompaniment on a beaten-up rehearsal room piano and within two bars Clinton murmured: 'Hey, man, you've got the touch.'

Colin assembled an onstage band with Ray Crane (trumpet), Trevor Whiting (saxes), Jim Richardson (bass) and Brian Abrahams of District 6 fame (drums). They became known as Colin Purbrook and his Clouds of Joy.

One evening in the bar I discovered, to my delight, that Colin had once depped for a week with Dr Crock and his Crackpots. The crazy bands of the thirties and forties – Spike Jones and his City Slickers in the USA, and their UK equivalents, Sid Seymour and his Mad Hatters, Sid Millward and his Nitwits and, of course, the Crackpots – have always seemed to me an area underexplored by musical historians.

As Colin told the story, he turned up at the theatre, a recent graduate with a degree in music from Cambridge University, and inquired after the whereabouts of his bandleader.

'He'll be in the pub.'

He went into the pub and there was Dr Crock, real name Harry Hines, and the conversation went:

'Harry Crock?'

'Yes.'
'I'm the piano player.'
'Can you play?'
'Yes.'
'Good. What will you have?'
The next time they met was onstage.

Colin taught me a great deal about the daily realities of a musician's life. Shirley and I were once having supper in a West End restaurant and, lo, there was Colin playing piano for the punters who, predictably, were totally ignoring him. It was reminiscent of a Bill Tidy cartoon in which the piano player says to a room full of loudly chattering diners: 'And now I'd like to play Jerome Kern's beautiful song "Choke you bastards, choke".' As we always do in these situations, we applauded each piece as loudly as possible, even encouraging one or two notional attempts at clapping from people at nearby tables, though mostly their hands didn't touch.

Afterwards we talked to Colin about the situation.

'Don't you mind they take no notice of you?'

He was totally phlegmatic. He had more phlegm in his soul than most people.

'Why should I mind?'

'Because they're a bunch of philistine, unappreciative zombies.'

'Look. If I wasn't working, what do you think I'd be doing?'

'Sitting at home?'

'Doing what?'

'Playing piano?'

'Right. So instead of that, I come here and play the piano. They give me some money and a free supper. Then I go home.'

Always quietly spoken, Colin lowered his voice a little more.

'And I'll let you into a secret. Once you've learned how to do it, playing music is the easiest way to make a living ever invented. But don't spread it around.'

He illustrated this with a story about getting a call to play in a recording session – he was a good reader and much in demand for studio work.

The message was: 'It's for a commercial and we want to recreate the Count Basie sound.'

'So I'll be Count Basie?'

'Right.'

Colin did the session and discovered, as he suspected, that his sole contribution was to replicate one of Basie's little three phrase fills at the end of the number.

'A full day in studio at union rates, and all I had to do was play six notes.'

'Colin, they weren't paying you for the six notes. To paraphrase James McNeill Whistler, they were paying you for a lifetime of experience.'

Colin raised one eyebrow slightly less than a millimetre: his way of signalling he had sniffed bullshit.

He was very proud of the fact that, of his year at Cambridge, he was the only one who had gone into jazz and the only one still working as a professional musician. As Clinton said, he had the touch: the touch of an angel.

Rent Party played to rave notices and packed houses. We broke the house records for the Theatre Royal but what gave me additional pleasure – and more than a little bit of pride – was that the stage was filled with black people and so was the auditorium. The energy flew back and forth and they were nights to treasure.

Key to the success was the lead given by Philip Hedley, especially in relation to race, which is a reality, and racism, which is a poison. The only way to deal with these things is to walk towards them.

That is why, when we all got together on the first day of rehearsals, I made a little speech. It went something like this.

'I'm a white guy from the North of England writing about Harlem. It's like James Baldwin writing a play about ship-building on the River Tyne. So here's the deal. If you think I've got anything wrong you look me in the eyes and say: Alan, you've got this wrong. And we'll fix it.'

It only happened once during the rehearsal period, when Clinton corrected me on a racial nuance of the plot, which I duly amended. The trade-off was I corrected him on a nuance of dialogue.

'Clinton, you've got a line about Louis Armstrong.'

'I know.'

'Well, I really think you would say Louis... pronouncing the S. I wouldn't but you would.'

'Louis. Got it, man.'

There was a lovely moment when we were compiling the blues medley. We wanted everybody to sing a blues made-to-measure for his or her special vocal qualities. Somewhere along the line, Pearly Gates suggested she might sing 'Stormy Weather'.

'It's a song I do in cabaret.'

'You can't sing "Stormy Weather", Pearly,' I said.

'Why not?'

'That's white man's music.'

Which sent her into near-hysterical laughter, rushing around the room telling everybody: 'Hey guys, you want to hear what Alan just said.'

The blues medley gave me the biggest kick during the show. It was launched by Clinton saying, in character, and paraphrasing Shakespeare:

'It's time for the blues at midnight.'

The challenge was to stop the audience applauding before the medley was completed.

'Do that,' I said, 'and it'll generate such an emotional charge the audience will blow the roof off at the end.'

And most nights, at the end of the twenty-five minutes of classic songs, the audience did exactly that.

There's an interesting technical note in the margins of the memory. Neither the performers nor the musicians were miked. The gospel of Purbrook prevailed: 'If there's too much noise, you can't hear the sound.'

Rent Party came within a whisker of a West End transfer – though in this case the whisker was twenty thousand pounds, that being the difference between what our producer raised and what he needed. But, as Shakespeare didn't quite say, the voyage of our lives is bound in hard-luck stories; and very boring they are too.

The show was very much a child of its time. In 2004 the Theatre Royal launched *The Big Life*, a Ska musical about the *Windrush* generation, which later moved into the West End. Written by Paul Sirett – another white guy – with music by Paul Joseph, it caught the imagination of the audience much as we had, but it also felt of a piece with the times that go on a-changing.

For a professional writer, the aftertaste of successful shows is often dominated, perversely, by the bits that didn't work. *A Very British Coup* was a political thriller that hoovered up most of the available awards in 1989. I often run the opening section at workshops and there's a line in it that never gets a laugh. A journalist, played by Keith

Allen, is released from prison, where he's been banged up for refusing to reveal his sources. He reports to his girlfriend that the experience hasn't been too bad and adds: 'Apparently you get a better cell if you're in BUPA.'

Nobody ever laughs. And I think it's funny, dammit.

There was a similar moment in *Rent Party*.

Polly Hemingway played a Thatcherite called Lady Sarah, who time-travels to Harlem in the belief that seeing these folk standing on their own two feet without resorting to help from a nanny state carries an important message for us all.

Once at the party she initially declines an offer of bootleg liquor and asks instead: 'Do you have any Malvern Water?'

This provokes the following chat among the party goers:

'Anybody know Malvern?'

'Malvern? What does he do?'

'He makes water.'

'Doesn't add up to a career.'

It should be no great secret by now that I'm fascinated, not to say obsessed, by comedy, humour, laughter and jokes. Though they overlap, the four are not precisely synonymous, though a full analysis requires a much longer book than this one. In 1997 the University of Northumbria gave me an honorary degree and, by way of thanks, I gave a lecture entitled: 'Seriously though – Old Jokes and the Zeitgeist.' It was a proper lecture with all the trappings, including a lectern.

Its central premise was that we define ourselves by what we laugh at, and if we don't laugh at anything, we're in deep trouble. When we visited Ceausescu's Bucharest our guide told us things were so bad people had stopped making jokes. QED.

Admittedly, many of my favourite jokes reinforce stereotypes and that's supposed to be a bad thing though I'm not entirely convinced: there's generally a morsel of truth hiding inside and we all believe in truth, don't we?

Here are some samples from the tray.

A Yorkshireman's comment on a top American comedian: 'He's all right, if you like laughing.'

Well, I'm pretty sure it was in that beautiful and noble county that someone asked me: 'Have you ever written anything funny?'

Or consider the Geordie, asked why he got married: 'Well, I was lonely after my bulldog died.'

The real-life parallel was a Newcastle taxi-driver who told us: 'I'm in deep clag. My wife's found out I've been having an affair. Mind you, it's my own fault. The family couldn't understand why I kept smiling all the time.'

Every professional writer's favourite is the one about the Irish actress who wanted the star part in the movie, so slept with the screenwriter.

I can't offer an exact parallel but it was in Dublin that a taxi-driver (always one of the truest barometers of a nation's psyche) gave us the following routine:

'Oh, the traffic in Dublin, it gets worse. But the government's going to solve the problem. Your man tells us we've got to start driving on the other side of the road. But we'll do it in stages, gradually you see, over a period, to be sure it's going to work. First the buses, then the taxis, then the trucks and then the private cars.'

'Sounds good,' we said.

'I told an American last week and he said: "But surely that isn't going to work".'

Jazz, naturally, is rich with such tales.

A doctor tells a jazz musician he's only got a month to live.

'On what?'

That story needs no explanation or justification.

Humour in jazz – i.e. within the music – is a much trickier proposition. Someone once said to me that the only truly funny tune ever written was the Laurel and Hardy cuckoo theme. I don't agree but it's a good debating point.

While living in Hull I was a member of the Jazz Record Society, a couple of dozen devotees who met in a room above a pub in the Old Town and played music to each other, very loudly, to the irritation of the people in the bar downstairs.

They asked me to give a talk and I chose the subject 'Humour in Jazz'. Among the pieces I played were Clark Terry's 'Mumbles' and a lovely track, drawn to my attention by jazz critic and writer, Bruce Crowther, where Memphis Slim sings 'Beer Drinking Woman' and Madeleine Gautier does a line-by-line translation into French: 'Elle était une grand buveure du bière. . .' It's bliss, if you can find it.

For the grand finale I chose Carla Bley's band playing 'Spangled Banner Minor and Other Patriotic Themes'. This is an extended piece – a kind of fantasia on national anthems – and lurches into some very wild free blowing before getting back on the rails just in time for a big and funny finish.

The band was at its loudest and wildest when I heard someone in the audience murmur to the bloke next to her: 'You're the president – can't you stop it?'

I laced my introductions with pertinent quotes from the great Whitney Balliett. On Johnny Hodges: 'Hodges makes his entry, sinuous and erotic, like a cat on the prowl. . .' – only to reveal at the end that I'd invented all the quotes myself.

Then as now, people have no idea about the things that go on in Hull on a Thursday night, especially when it's raining.

What I couldn't have anticipated was that a few years later I'd end up writing and presenting two Radio 3 series on these very themes: *Humour in Jazz* and *Carla Bley*. This was as a result of meeting Derek Drescher, a fine and quietly reckless BBC producer whose reward for keeping an eye on *Desert Island Discs* for a long period, was to be given a relatively free hand in jazz broadcasting; or maybe it wasn't a free hand and he was just too quick on his feet for middle management. Whatever the truth of the matter, when he left the BBC, he bequeathed to them a treasure trove of recorded performances and interviews, notably those conducted by Charles Fox, with most of the greatest players of our music.

Our first meeting with Carla Bley was in Paris, where she was working with her partner, Steve Swallow. We recorded an interview to bookend a concert she was to give in Glasgow and I was able to write in the diary: 'Lunch in Paris with Carla.'

Later, when we did the radio series, she came to our flat in Chalk Farm to record an extended interview. She and Steve were on the road with the big band and when she called to finalise the arrangements she said to Shirley: 'We haven't been long enough any place to do any washing. We're running out of clean clothes.'

'Bring everything with you,' said Shirley. 'We can run the washing machine while you talk to Alan.'

So, while Carla and I had in-depth discussions about the music, Shirley supervised the laundry in another room. It's probably never like that for Madonna or the Rolling Stones.

Her conversation is much like her music – quirky, knowledgeable, constantly taking you by surprise. On the influence of Kurt Weill: 'The amazing thing is, I was influenced by him before I'd even heard his music.' On closer inspection, we agreed all composers – like writers – are subjected to influences without necessarily knowing at the time where they originated. It's only in retrospect these things become clear. This has a wider application: consider all those people driving Picasso cars and wearing Charles Rennie Mackintosh earrings. Artists – like dog-shit – get everywhere.

HI – I'M ON THE TERRAIN
(POST-MODERN MINIMALIST JOKE)

One day Carla and I were comparing notes about professional expertise. I made the point that, having written so much in so many forms, I had a bank of knowledge that I could draw upon any time. If I wrote myself into a tight corner, I could generally find a way out because I'd been there before in another play. Was it the same for composers and musicians?

'Yes,' said Carla, 'but if I listen to old recordings, I can't help thinking I was more interesting when I didn't know so much.'

It was a brilliant observation: the old business of the innocent eye and the child's vision. The ability to see what is in front of you, not what the world has told you is there. Or, to express it another way, the only true sophistication is simplicity: whether it's a Picasso line drawing, a Laurel and Hardy sight gag or, to go back the very beginning, Duke Ellington's 'Mood Indigo'.

It's also vital to note that these excellent adventures involving jazz, humour, Derek Drescher and Carla Bley took place in radio and, not only that, but BBC radio. Hiding inside the BBC is a strange, old-fashioned idea called public service broadcasting.

Politicians and – to their shame – senior broadcasters often seem confused about what public service broadcasting means. It's very simple. It means placing the needs of the audience first. By comparison, commercial broadcasting (or 'independent' to use the conventional euphemism) places the needs of the shareholders first.

Needs, in this debate, are not the same as wants. What I want from television is trustworthy news, a few good laughs and decent coverage of my preferred sports: football, cricket and snooker. Beyond those basic items we need to be taken by surprise. We didn't know we needed the plays of Jack Rosenthal, John Hopkins and Dennis Potter until we saw them; but looking back, it's impossible to imagine a world without them. The same applies, to take a couple of home-grown examples, to the music of Stan Tracey and Joe Harriott. We didn't *want* Stan's *Under Milk Wood* suite, or Joe's experiments in free-form, but they satisfied a profound need.

That's why the current obsession with research and focus groups is a self-fulfilling catastrophe. The best this approach can deliver is a crude estimate of what people think they want. It can never measure human needs, which are complex and contradictory; that's what makes them human. And all the blue-skies thinking and management jargon in the universe can't hope to analyse what happens when a musician sits down at a piano, a painter picks up a brush or a writer attacks a blank sheet of paper. This is probably the reason John Birt and I don't exchange Christmas cards.

By some miracle, radio has escaped some of the vandalism inflicted on other areas of the BBC. As with most established institutions, it helps if you are operating well away from London. Distance from headquarters adds enchantment.

Over the last decade I've worked in both radio and television for BBC Wales in Cardiff, and that is exactly the kind of oasis where creativity is still able to flourish. My best friend at the Welsh court is radio producer, Alison Hindell. She was recently appointed Head of Radio Drama at the BBC, thus vindicating what I hope I said when we first met: 'Stick with me, kid, and I'll make you into a star.' It's what I say to all of the women I work with, and some of the men.

Around the turn of the century Alison approached me with a tempting bundle of research material from the Swansea Women's Jazz Archive, assembled by the heroic efforts of local historian and musician, Jen Wilson. Did I think there might be a play, or a series, hiding inside? I had a quick glance and there was.

There were two outstanding stories in the research, both of them holding out their hands and saying: write me! The

first centred around the Fisk Jubilee Singers, a choir originally formed by students of Fisk University in Nashville,
Tennessee. The university had been set up in 1866 as a centre for the education of newly-emancipated slaves. Being
such a good cause it was naturally broke and, as a response
to the situation, the choir went on the road to raise money,
and became world-famous in the process. In this country
they appeared in front of Queen Victoria and William
Gladstone but, more helpfully for our purposes, in South
Wales.

Their official programme promised 'negro spirituals and
plantation melodies' and, in a country where choral singing
is valued on a par with life itself, the choir took the valleys
by storm.

The second fascinating element in the research material
was the tea-room phenomenon of the 1920s and '30s – what
you might called Kardomah Syndrome. Swansea apparently
had these on every High Street corner, all with live music –
a light orchestra playing popular songs of the day – and,
vital to our purpose, the musicians were almost all women.
The shortage of male musicians was a bleak side-effect of
the First World War, the one they called Great.

Dramatically speaking, what I had on my hands was a
saga, starting in the late nineteenth century and ending in
the present day. Sagas can be tricky because the audience
has to remember who everybody is, how they are related to
everybody else and what year are we in anyway? I solved the
problem by focussing the narrative on five generations of
women, all called Megan, complete with regnal numbers –
from Megan the First to Megan the Fifth inclusive – and on
a piece of music.

There is a surviving 1913 recording of the Fisk Jubilee
Quartet, singing a spiritual called 'Roll Jordan Roll'. It is, in

all honesty, a pretty somnolent piece of work, starting with a simple four-note phrase – doh-me-soh-doh – and continuing in that vein for a while before livening up with a counter-melody. On the other hand, it meant we needn't be inhibited about kicking the stuffing out of it in the cause of drama, something you'd be less inclined to do with, say, the Bach *B Minor Mass*.

We ended up with a trilogy called *The Devil's Music*.

In Episode One, Megan the First hears Frederick Loudin's Fisk Singers, falls in love with their sound, and forms her own choir which scandalises the chapel elders with a stomping hand-clapping version of 'Oh Didn't the Lord Deliver Daniel', a splendid song which I found on an LP by the great Paul Robeson.

In Episode Two, Megan the Second, a piano player in a tea-room orchestra and bored out of her skull, remembers a tune her mother used to sing called 'Roll Jordan Roll' and recycles it as a comic number called 'Williams' Pork Pies'. Here's a poignant fragment:

> Williams' pork pies
> Fatten your thighs
> A word to the wise
> You'll achieve a vast size
> With Williams' pork pies
>
> This little piggy goes wee-wee-wee
> As he must
> This little piggy can see-see-see
> Under the crust
>
> Williams' pork pies
> Tell you no lies
> You can hear piggy's cries

> You can hear piggy's sighs
> In Williams' pork pies.

Naturally, this being a play, she sings the song on the very day that Mr Williams, the pork pie manufacturer, is present and taking tea. Megan is sacked on the spot. This motif – subversive mischief followed by instant dismissal – pops up at regular intervals in my work and probably conceals a mortal terror of having a proper job.

In the third play, Megan the Fifth is – would you believe? – a jazz guitarist from Swansea. She's practising for a gig at the Brecon Festival. She plays a little riff which grandma, Megan the Third, recognises as the 'Roll Jordan Roll' theme, but the young woman can't remember where she heard it. It just fell out of her head, into her fingers and on to the frets.

At Brecon she meets an American sax player called Frederick Loudin. He is a direct descendant of the original. They go up into the Brecon Beacons and play the tune together. She returns the music to its spiritual owner.

That's the tale in essence. Along the way we explored all the best historical themes as they came along: women's suffrage, the General Strike and the Depression, two World Wars and race. As Eric Morecambe used to say: 'We're getting them all in tonight, Ern.'

The music for the trilogy was written and arranged by Paula Gardiner, a bass player who lives in one of the valleys – not only that, she and her bloke have got their own church hall – where they live – and a church, which they're planning to transform into something to do with art.

There was an extra chapter to the story when Paula's band – a cool, post-bop quintet – appeared at the Brecon Festival and, in the time-honoured phrase, they played our tune. Art echoing life echoing art echoing life and so on.

Or, as Trevor Chaplin might say, just listen to the music and don't ask too many stupid questions.

I think it was Thomas Beecham who said: the English don't like music but they like the noise it makes.

This crosses my mind every time I manage to sneak jazz into any form of drama, whether radio, television or stage. We are told at regular intervals, by various spokespersons in the media, that the public doesn't like jazz. Yet our music is used for all kinds of nefarious purposes, the shabbiest example being television commercials. Nina Simone achieved a late burst of fame when 'My Baby Just Cares for Me' was used to sell something or other. I've also heard everybody from Billie Holiday to Charles Mingus being abused in this fashion; though I make it a firm rule not to buy any of the products advertised in this way.

Jazz, in other words, crops up all over the place, and people will invariably get along with it, as long as you don't tell them what it is. Let them trust their ears. We had a startling example of this in 1990 with a stage play called *Going Home*, presented by Live Theatre at the Playhouse in Newcastle. It was yet another simple tale, inspired by a trip Shirley and I took to Australia in 1988, where I spent three months as Writer-in-Residence at the Film, Television and Radio School in Sydney, with side-trips to Perth, Melbourne and Brisbane.

My central character is a Geordie called Bob – played by Tim Healy – back on a visit from Australia to see family and friends. He is horrified by what he discovers: the greed, intolerance and vulgarity released by Thatcherism.

It is, naturally, a comedy.

My director, Max Roberts – the best of good guys and

the dearest of friends destined, though we didn't know it at the time, to become my son-in-law and father of two spectacular grandsons – asked about the music.

'Yes, Max, we'll have some music. I've mentioned it in the script.'

'How about live music?'

'Can we afford live music?'

'Yes.'

'Wow.'

'I thought we might approach Ian Carr.'

'Seriously?'

'Yes. You know him, don't you?'

'Yes. We were students together.'

'OK?'

'OK.'

Working with Max has always been like that. We don't blether on endlessly about relationships, character arcs and first act turning points. Like Duke, we believe that too much talk stinks up the place. That's why we've worked together happily for twenty years.

Ian Carr, of course, had a long-time association with Newcastle. After student days he and his brother Mike formed the EmCee Five who startled the music world in the early sixties with a highly personal and original brand of Tyneside bop.

He's also highly literate with acclaimed biographies of Miles Davis and Keith Jarrett to his name. It isn't compulsory but it does help if a musical collaborator can read a script and figure out what you're on about.

The musical requirements of *Going Home* were quite different from the norm. For a start there were no songs. But there were lots of musical references in the stage directions and dialogue. It would take too long to explain why, but for reasons of plot characters talked of people like Duke Ellington and Coleman Hawkins.

Ian composed a series of pieces that acted like a film score, underlining the moments, adding texture to the action, and played them onstage along with Lewis Watson (saxes), Paul Flush (piano), Adrian Tilbrook (drums) and Peter Ayton (bass).

But it wasn't that simple. It never is.

Audiences react in different ways on different nights. It was a comedy so sometimes they laughed in the right places, sometimes in the wrong places and sometimes not at all.

What Ian and the band did was extraordinary. When the name Duke Ellington was mentioned, we heard an instant Ellingtonian quote on trumpet – likewise Coleman Hawkins – and so on throughout the play. By definition, there was no knowing in advance precisely when these moments would be. The guys had to listen intently, pick the moment, play the phrase and still, in the great musicial tradition, finish level. Only jazz musicians would be capable of doing it.

After a couple of performances I said to Ian:

'You realise what you're doing is impossible?'

'Is it?'

'Yes.'

'It might be better if you don't tell me.'

Audiences loved the play and they loved the music though my guess is that had you conducted a poll with the question 'Do you like modern jazz?' a majority would have said, no, they didn't.

That's the wonderful thing about music: it can be described but not explained. To recycle the tiresome old advertising slogan, it reaches the parts other art forms can't reach. We had another telling example in 1995, at the Theatre Royal in Newcastle, in a play called *Shooting the Legend*. Max Roberts directed, Tim Healy starred and this time we had an array of songs including a stand-out performance by Tim of 'Mustang Sally'; a Tamla Motown medley featuring Libby Davison (later of *The Bill*); Charlie Hardwicke (later of *Emmerdale*); Denise Welch (later of *Coronation Street*); and an all-join-in audience participation version of a nineteenth century Geordie song called 'Wor Nanny's A Mazer'.

A local theatre-goer said to me one night: 'Naebody's ganna confuse you with Ibsen or Strindberg, bonny lad.'

Because we thought people might not be familiar with 'Wor Nanny' we arranged for front-of-house staff to scatter song sheets among the audience, containing the words to the chorus:

> And ay wor Nanny's a Mazer and a mazer she remains,
> An' as lang as Aa live Aa winnet forget the day we lost the trains.

The revelation was the number of people who said to me afterwards: 'You know what? I knew the song already. But I don't ever remember learning it.'

Out of that experience I drew a tentative conclusion about the nature of drama and maybe of all the arts. The challenge is to put on the stage or on the screen something that reminds the audience of a music they once knew and thought they had forgotten.

It helps to achieve this if the play-makers can hang on to the innocence and the child's vision and, at the same time, ignore the people who tell you – you can't do that, it's impossible. One of about three things I remember from my architectural training is Le Corbusier's dictum: that which gives our dreams their daring is that they can be realised.

Enough. I'm starting to stink up the place.

Throwing Out the Vinyl Blues

When I was researching *The Devil's Music* I went into the living room one day to play Paul Robeson's song, 'Oh Didn't the Lord Deliver Daniel'. A young woman – let's say mid-thirties – who had called in to cut our hair, stared at me and said: 'You're playing a record.'

'Yes,' I said. 'It's called an LP. They used to be all the rage.'

She had clearly never seen such a thing in her life. It was as if she'd seen me riding along the street on a penny-farthing bicycle. It was the incident that prompted the following song.

Oddly enough, since writing it, vinyl and even shellac have been making something of a comeback. I've also discovered why it is that some LPs sound better than their CD equivalents. In the olden days, sound engineers used their ears, instead of digital aids. Am I alone in finding digital technology a bit creepy? I have this Orwellian nightmare of a future in which babies will be born with genetically implanted bar codes and pin numbers.

But this is what I wrote about vinyl.

> Got the throwing out the vinyl
> Throwing out the vinyl blues
> My decision's final
> It's the throwing out the vinyl blues
> Songs for swinging vicars
> Duke plays Doris Day
> Spike Jones City Slickers
> Live at Monterey
> Kenny Baker's dozen
> Loussier plays Bach

Woody Herman's cousin
At the Pizza on the Park
You can hear it on the network news
I'm slinging out the vinyl blues

Got the throwing out the vinyl
Throwing out the vinyl blues
Irrevocable – final
I'm throwing out the vinyl blues
Ella sings Rolf Harris
Rolf plays Sonny Stitt
Django live in Paris
Des O'Connor's hit
Carla's Escalator
Aretha Franklin's soul
Made into a plate or
An ornamental bowl
You can see me on the network news
Re-cycling all my vinyl blues

Got the throwing out the vinyl
Throwing out the vinyl blues
With courage intestinal
I'm throwing out the vinyl blues
Live at the Apollo
Andy's Clouds of Joy
They're about to follow
The best of Harry Roy
Humphrey, Chris and Acker
They find it really hard
Get their tickets from the knacker
Then he takes them to his yard
You'll see them on the network news

The throwing out the vinyl blues
Irrevocable – final
With courage intestinal
Down the old urinal
I'm flushing out the vinyl blues

8.

Sweethearts on Parade

One of the phrases that recurs in *Doggin' Around* is 'a sweet guy and a very dear friend' which the pianist, Joe Warren, uses in reference to every jazz musician in the history of the music, especially those he's never met. This probably reflects some deep-seated psychological quirk in my own nature. I've always tended to like people, whatever the evidence that tells me I shouldn't. Maybe for this reason, critics have occasionally found my work 'soft-centred' – a cardinal sin, apparently, in a world where it's almost compulsory to be materialistic and cynical.

Needless to say, I have theories about this. At my age I have theories about everything, from Darwin's origin of species to the offside rule. For what it's worth, my theory of humanity goes like this. I believe the majority of people would rather be decent, kind and honourable, given the choice and an even break. They only become tough and ruthless when they're acting on behalf of an institution, and put on a real or imaginary uniform. Wars only work if the troops wear contrasting costumes, so they all know which direction to aim the guns. If they turned up on the battlefield in their tee-shirts and jeans, the conflict would soon degenerate into chaos and confusion, somebody would produce a football or a guitar or a bottle of the hard stuff – preferably all three – civilisation would be resumed and the generals would have to find proper jobs.

Even in the relatively peaceful context of everyday existence the same rules apply. Senior television executives who, in their home life are no doubt decent people who cherish their families and their dogs, love to prove their ruthless decision-making prowess by sacking people: not because they believe this will make the world any better, but because they believe that's what the institution requires. Watch any movie about high-level movers and shakers, especially in the USA, and the message is clear: the sharper the suit, the nastier the man.

Now, I daresay there are leading players in the Mafia who actually get job satisfaction from protection rackets and related skulduggery, including bouts of homicide, but my gut instinct says that even they, given the choice, would find greater fulfilment as playwrights or piano players. Maybe Sinatra was in hock to the mob, but it was a two-way transaction. Every man of that generation – including the mobsters – wanted to be Sinatra. The next best thing was to be photographed with him.

All this is by way of justification for my claim that in my universe there is no shortage of sweet guys and very dear friends, both male and female; and the playwright, Jack Rosenthal, could lay claim to being one of the sweetest and dearest. His plays demonstrated this. There isn't an evil person in any of them. There are weak people and flawed people, but there are no bad people. Their tragi-comic dilemmas invariably derive from failed attempts to be good.

For some years we were both represented by the same

agent, the wild and wilful Peggy Ramsay. Peggy died in 1992 but I have her picture hanging on the wall and she continues to talk to me, offering her special brand of ruthless advice.

'Do you really have to deal with these people, darling? They're so utterly vulgar. And if you must go whoring in Hollywood, insist on the going rate, spread your legs and give good value.'

One of her many unique habits was to talk about her clients behind their backs. If one of us had a play on, she would talk to everybody else about it first, before taking on the actual writer. My best guess is that she used us all as a sounding-board to work out what she herself really thought. This led to the only occasion when I won an argument with her: my sole victory in thirty years.

She called me one day to talk about a play of Jack's which had been on the previous evening.

'Did you see Jack's play, darling?'

'Naturally.'

'I've just realised something. You two are so alike.'

'Are we?'

'Yes, dear. You both love to write about failure.'

'Wrong, Peggy.'

'Wrong!'

The telephone vibrated. So did the universe.

'Why am I wrong?'

'We don't write about failure. We write about the dignity of failure.'

There was a long silence. I braced myself.

'You're quite right, dear. Do forgive me.'

In the matter of nice people behaving badly, it's worth noting that Peggy could be tough, ruthless and cynical but she was acting on behalf of her institution – a stable of highly-gifted playwrights. Since, in her passionate view, writers were the most important people in the history of the world, she had a sturdy moral foundation for her stance.

One day in 1988, Jack called me with a proposition. Even then – and things are much worse now – he was concerned about the decline in the single-shot television play. He was constantly dreaming up ways of smuggling these back on to the screen and he'd come up with an idea.

'It'll be a six-part series called *Article For Sale*. Channel Four are interested. Six different writers. Six original plays. Sixty minutes long. But somewhere in the story somebody buys or sells something second-hand. And that's the excuse for the play.'

'Sounds great. Put me down for a tenor saxophone.'

That's where I started. Somebody buys or sells a tenor. But who? In these situations the obvious strategy is to do the least obvious thing and, at the risk of drifting into stereotypes about sweet old ladies, I decided my central character should be a grey-haired woman in her sixties. I called her Elizabeth, in honour of the wonderful Elizabeth Welch, whom we'd recently seen giving a majestic perform-ance at the Almeida Theatre.

But why should she want a tenor in the first place? Easy. She played in an all-women dance band during the war only to quit playing in 1945 when she met and married a dull bank manager husband. He's now retired and sits at home all day juggling his shares, while she's going crazy with bore-dom.

She buys the tenor from a second-hand shop and starts clandestine busking, well away from home so as not to be detected. In the course of the action she meets the young black musician who's had to hock the instrument in the first place, discovers he's ten times the player she is, and gives it back to him. Meanwhile – and in drama there's always a meanwhile – she's also been spotted by Patrick, an old friend from the war who briefly played drums in the band while wearing women's clothes, thus avoiding the call-up.

At the end of the play the busker is back on his regular gig, blowing superbly: husband is happily playing with his shares; and Elizabeth and Patrick meet once a week in the park to feed the ducks and talk about old times.

By my standards it was pretty action-packed stuff and the front office was very happy with the piece. I started assembling my dream cast. It included Brenda Bruce, on the evidence of a cracking performance we'd seen her give in a Shirley Gee play at Hampstead Theatre, and Alan Cooke, who had played Lester Young in *Prez*, and was a good tenor player in real life.

The excitement peaked and then petered out. Nothing happened for a while and went on happening for about five years. Jack reported to me about the problems with the broadcasters.

'They only like three of the plays.'

'Yours, mine and one other?'

'Obviously.'

It's possible this generous-spirited man said the same to all the other writers but the nub of it was that the companies only wanted three of the plays, and Jack was insistent they do all six or none at all.

The keen-eyed executives in their sharp suits grasped the nettle with post-Thatcherite zeal. None at all was the answer. It had the smack of firm decision-making about it and people were being given knighthoods for this kind of unsentimental ruthlessness.

My attitude to rejection has always been the same. I

swear and stamp my foot for twenty minutes or so, and then say sod it and get on with something else. But this time I wasn't allowed to.

After Peggy Ramsay died, I linked up with a new agent, Alexandra Cann. Alex is an Australian from Sydney, and therefore totally free of Anglo-Saxon bullshit. She inherited a chaotic mess of paper from Peggy's office but, going through it with due diligence, came across the play under its then title, *Body and Soul*.

'This is too good to waste,' she said.

'Is it? I think I was planning to waste it.'

'Why don't you expand it? Turn it into a full-length screenplay.'

'Like a proper movie?'

'Exactly like a proper movie.'

I wrote the extended screenplay version in 1997, immediately after a teaching trip to Copenhagen which coincided with Tony Blair's first election win. The euphoria of seeing Portillo and Co. bite the dust went some way to compensate for the surprising apathy of the students at the film school. It might have been my fault for not being cutting edge enough but we'll never know. File under: it really doesn't matter any more.

One of the more cheerful aspects of our trip was visiting the Tivoli Gardens where, one very chilly May evening, we heard a big band playing old-style swing arrangements. The playing was efficient rather than inspired, though that might have been the temperature. We could see the notes emerging from the brass section in vapour form.

But it isn't entirely coincidental that in the first version of what was now called *The Last of the Blonde Bombshells*, the climactic concert took place at the Tivoli Gardens, complete with a firework display and some strolling elephants, both of which we'd seen during our visit. The elephants, incidentally, were on leads and accompanied by minders, since they are not native to Denmark.

All this visual tomfoolery was part of a larger strategy called 'opening up the screenplay'. There's a curious mythology to the business of screenwriting. It's generally believed that television is about people in rooms talking to each other; whereas big movies are about the same people running up and down burning buildings, galloping across plains, cutting their way through jungles, or crawling across deserts, while shouting much the same sort of dialogue at each other that they would have said in the rooms, if they'd bothered to stay home. This is an over-simplification, but the fact remains that the decision-makers tend to judge screenplays by the amount of money visible on the page.

Big movies spend a lot of money and flaunt it. Television plays spend as little as possible and try not to be caught out.

We eventually made *Blonde Bombshells* for television, with a large budget thanks to the participation of the American company, HBO, in the year 2000. Along the way we had three or four producers, eighteen versions of the screenplay, and the film reached the screen twelve years after Jack Rosenthal's original phone call saying: 'I've had an idea.' Round about the fifth draft the Tivoli Gardens fell out of the story, along with the fireworks and the elephants.

The keys that helped unlock the doors of the vaults where production money is stored were provided by Dame Judi Dench and Sir Ian Holm. They both fell in love with the screenplay at an early stage. When Dame Cleo Laine joined the cast I started the rumour that I was only pre-pared to work with titled actors, though I later relented, as who wouldn't when presented with Olympia Dukakis, June

BUT THERE'S STILL ONE THING I DON'T
UNDERSTAND, INSPECTOR,

(GRAND OLD DIALOGUE REVISITED)

Whitfield, Joan Sims, Leslie Caron and Billie Whitelaw.

I adopted a cute line of dialogue when questioned about this remarkable galaxy of talent. When asked: 'How did you assemble such an amazing cast?' I'd say: 'We sent them the screenplay.'

The best memories from the making of the film are, inevitably, musical: Cleo singing 'When the World Was Young', unaccompanied, at the first readthrough and leaving an entire rehearsal room in tears: the friendship that developed between June Whitfield and Pete Strange, who taught June how to look as if she was really playing a trombone; and the similar relationship that developed between Judi and Kathleen Stobart, the designated tenor sax coach.

The BBC, naturally enough, saw the piece as a family movie and this produced a clutch of dilemmas. The opening scene shows Elizabeth at her husband's funeral. In accordance with his wishes, 'My Way' is played, at which point she mutters: 'I hate this fucking song.' But you're not supposed to use that word in a family movie, even though it's shown after the nine o'clock watershed. In our case it would have been about five past nine, the greyest of grey areas. The request came: could we change the line? Always eager to please I suggested: 'I hate this sodding song,' though I was a bit unhappy about the double-s sound. It then turned out that it was this particular line that sold the screenplay to Judi in the first place. She just wanted to say that line. The fuck stayed, with an official BBC health warning on the night.

The other problem was 'My Way'. I feel exactly the same way about it as my central character, which is why I gave her the line in the first place. On the other hand, millions of people love it, including, I imagine, Paul Anka and the Sinatra estate. After endless, pointless, time-consuming debates, we ended up with 'Magic Moments' though in the American version, HBO opted, bizarrely, for 'A Wandering Minstrel I' from the Gilbert and Sullivan songbook. I had a few perplexed emails from friends in the States, asking what G & S ever did to upset me.

Multiply these little local difficulties by about a hundred, and you'll have a fair idea of the fun and games that went into the making of the film. It's much the same with any other film. Only the names change.

The Last of the Blonde Bombshells was shown in 2000, was well-reviewed and well-liked, Judi collected her annual BAFTA award, we all preened ourselves and I prepared to get on with something entirely different. Except I didn't.

A New York producer – and there's a phrase to quicken the senses and summon up the blood – decided *Blonde Bombshells* would make a good stage musical and commissioned me to write a version for the theatre. Over the next couple of years, without neglecting my other duties – grandchildren, family life in general, Hull City, Ronnie's, earning a living – I wrote two or three drafts.

In fairness, what I produced gave problems. It wasn't on the scale of conventional West End musicals, nor was it in that style. A story about a World War Two dance band getting together to play again in, let's say, late middle age, was never going to turn out like *Les Miserables* or *Phantom of the Opera*. It was an open question whether we could sell it to the public as a musical at all. It was actually a play about musicians, playing and singing in the course of the action. We had meetings, in London and New York, to discuss all this. The overall conclusion was that it was a tough sell. Everybody loved the script; the problem was picking a label to hang around its neck that would make sense to the coach parties from Essex and the tourists from one-horse towns in America.

After a lot of coming and going, I ended up with a version that needed a cast of twenty-four, mostly women, all of them able to play instruments and sing songs. The women had to be in two batches of eight – the same characters, with a fifty year gap between – plus a token handful of supplementary blokes.

The eventual game plan was to open the show at the West Yorkshire Playhouse in Leeds in April 2004, and then move on to the West End. After that, trailing clouds of glory, we'd be off to Broadway, followed by every major city in the world, not to mention every conurbation in the universe, including those in galaxies not yet discovered.

But the theatre – which, in many ways, closely resembles life – isn't like that. Exactly a month before the start of rehearsals, our New York producer phoned Alexandra, my agent, to say everything was fine with the deal but, by the way, could I reduce the cast from twenty-four to twelve?

This was not good news. We concluded that he wanted to break the deal. He succeeded.

I took the next available train to Leeds and had crisis talks with Ian Brown, artistic director of the Playhouse. In summary, our conversation ran something like this:

'I assume the theatre can't afford twenty-four actors, Ian?'

'Not for one show.'

'But you've already promised the people of Leeds a show more or less concerned with a band called the Blonde Bombshells?'

'Yes.'

'Which gives us a problem.'

'Yes.'

'How many actors can you afford?'

'Ten.'

'OK. I'll write a show for ten actors. It'll be called...'

There was a pause Samuel Beckett wouldn't have been ashamed of.

'...*Blonde Bombshells of 1943.*'

We shook hands on the deal. Whereas the original was about a group of older people getting together to re-capture their lost youth, the new play would be mostly about the young band and the experience of playing in wartime conditions.

For all practical purposes it was a brand-new play and I had a month to write it. This is less of a problem than some people might imagine. Noel Coward apparently wrote *Private Lives* over a weekend and in the days when Alan Ayckbourn only wrote one play a year (he's speeded up since, in order to overtake Shakespeare) he claimed that he thought about each play for fifty weeks and wrote it in a fortnight.

The main frustration was the lack of time to do proper research into the wartime experience of professional musicians. This came into sharp focus when I interviewed Kathleen Stobart for a *Guardian* article run to coincide with the opening of the show.

Kathy, a Tynesider like me, was born in South Shields and was working at Greenwoods the Printers – for my Uncle Joe, as it happens, but Joe is at least three other stories for another day, or maybe a late night – when she saw an advertisement saying Don Rico needed a tenor sax player for his Ladies Swing Band.

She borrowed her brother's tenor sax – 'I'd been learning about two years' – went to Sunderland for her audition and was asked to play from a piece of sheet music.

'He said: you're not really very good, are you? Do you do anything else? I said: yes, I've been in concert parties since I was nine, at miners' welfares and seamen's missions and such. So I sang and I danced, went into the old tap step, and did my impersonations of ZaSu Pitts and Gracie Fields.'

She was given the job at 8s. 6d. a week plus board and lodging. It was a shilling more than she'd been paid at the printers and in the early years of the war found herself playing twice-nightly variety on the Moss Empires music-hall circuit with the swing band which, she says, 'swung like a bucket of lead.'

'We visited all kinds of places that were being bombed and if there was a raid on after the show was over, we would continue with a band show. And I was up there dancing and impersonating and pulling the roof down because I was a kid, only fourteen and a half. Like a long string bean I was.'

Kathy later worked at the Oxford Galleries dance hall in Newcastle (one of our student haunts in the 1950s) where, in addition to the regular dances every evening – old time on Thursdays – she played afternoon tea dances and Sunday concerts at a cinema in the city.

'I was playing eleven times a week. If you can't learn doing that you're never going to learn.'

At this time she met Keith Bird, a London-based jazz musician serving in the RAF and passing through the North-East. He introduced her to jazz, coaching her during the tea breaks.

'He'd play a chord on the piano and say: play what you can hear in there. I could feel my fingers buzzing on the beat. He found out I had perfect pitch. And that was it.'

Bird encouraged her to move to London and take over his regular job playing with a quartet at the Montague Ballroom in Ealing. She soon slipped into a routine, rushing away after her Ealing job – 'they used to let me off the last waltz' – taking the underground to play late night jazz at the Jamboree Club in Wardour Street, Soho, in a band led by a jazz trumpet player called Denis Rose.

'We'd play till five in the morning and if there was an air raid we'd keep on going. Denis used to say, "If you hear anything funny dive under the piano... A building can fall on a grand piano."'

It was here that she met the Canadian pianist and bandleader, Art Thompson, her first husband. She was a member of his band when it moved into the prestigious Embassy Club, though not without opposition from the management.

'They said: "We'll have problems right away, a woman in the band, all those people hanging round, soldiers, problems right away."'

The solution was to dress her exactly like the rest of the band, in a tuxedo with a skirt instead of the trousers.

Such trouble as there was came not because of her, nor the many stars who passed through the club – Glenn Miller, Bing Crosby, Clark Gable, David Niven, Bob Hope and the Andrews Sisters, among others – but from the young RAF pilots in the balcony above the bandstand who used to take flying leaps over the heads of the musicians on to the dance floor.

Her most poignant memory is of the night Glenn Miller, normally the most modest of drinkers, got drunk. They noticed him sitting for the first time ever with a glass full of whisky in his hand and found him, much later, propped up against a wall, 'absolutely legless'.

'We took him down this alley in Piccadilly, we nearly dragged him, and the waiter had a taxi there and Art pushed Glenn into the back seat, gave the driver ten bob and said, "Please take this officer to such-and-such a club." And that was it. Pow. Next thing we knew was that Glenn had taken off for Paris ahead of his band... and nobody ever saw him again. We were among the last people to see him.'

Like many of her generation, she looks back on the war as the best of times and the worst of times. She remembers the 'camaraderie, the miles of hoses, that funny burning smell and dust in the air where the buildings had fallen' and the airmen who came into the club asking, 'Can Kathy sing "Shoo-Shoo-Baby" for us because we're expecting our new Dakota in and we're going to name her *Shoo-Shoo-Baby*.'

'And I believe they did paint a blonde lady on the front with a saxophone and underneath it, *Shoo-Shoo-Baby*.'

It was deeply frustrating to hear all these stories from Kathy after I'd written the play, though I'm working on a new version – even cheaper than the Leeds production – and might sneak some of them in on this occasion. The consolation prize was sitting in the theatre on the first night of *Blonde Bombshells of 1943*, with Shirley on one side and Kathy on the other. It got even better when our onstage band played the first number and Kathy grasped my arm in excitement and whole-hearted approval.

At the end of the show, with Dilys Laye and John Woodvine as the senior citizens presiding over the story, and the eight-piece Blonde Bombshells of 1943 swinging Trummy Young's 'T'Ain't Whatcha Do', every foot in the audience was tapping and once again nobody was getting me confused with Ibsen or Strindberg – nor, for that matter, with Ivor Novello or Andrew Lloyd Webber.

And if that wasn't glory enough, the next morning Kathy and I were on *Woman's Hour* to talk about it all.

Interwoven with the long-running *Blonde Bombshells* saga I slotted in another couple of stage plays with significant musical content and world-famous collaborators: John Dankworth and Sir Peter Maxwell Davies.

The Dankworth connection was for a play called *The Last Days of the Empire*, written for the Watermill Theatre in Newbury which, over the last twenty years, has been one of the bravest and most enterprising theatres in the land, specialising in radical productions of Shakespeare and audacious musicals, including a version of *The Gondoliers* with eight actors playing all the parts, singing all the songs and playing all the music. The Watermill was definitely my kind of theatre.

The play was a spin-off from an abandoned project written for Lenny Henry in the early 1990s – a story about

a young man called Rudy, a Jamaican of the *Windrush* generation. In Jamaica he's a policeman by day and sings like Nat
King Cole every evening. He arrives in England, goes to the
Labour Exchange and discovers a) there are no black
policemen and b) you don't get jobs singing like Nat King
Cole at the Labour Exchange. In the story he ends up working the music-hall circuit before joining a Latin-American
band, modelled on the Edmundo Ros Orchestra.

I became fascinated by Ros though admittedly I do fas-
cinate easily. Born in Trinidad, he was happy to be regarded
by the public as Venezuelan because it was more exotic and,
in fairness, he had spent some of his early years in that
country. Exploring the theme a little more, I remembered
the Hermanos Deniz Cuban Rhythm Band, run by the
remarkable Deniz brothers from Cardiff. I don't know
whether they'd ever been to Cuba though I do remember
seeing Laurie Deniz at the City Hall in Hull, playing high
quality bop guitar with the Ray Ellington Quartet.

Out of this melting pot emerged the idea of a totally
ersatz Latin-American band run in the 1950s by Mike and
Peggy Gorman, music-hall veterans from Solihull who,
in Coronation year, wrote a calypso and made the Hit
Parade. Bearing in mind that the Top Twenty of the period
was distinguished by such artists as the Singing Dogs and
the Chipmunks, it wasn't too far-fetched a notion. The
band is called Pedro Gonzales and his Caribbean Rhythm,
featuring song stylist, Enrico Olmedo, plus a bass player
from Leeds, a pianist from Glasgow and a drummer from
Stockton-on-Tees. It is likely that none of them has ever
been within ten thousand miles of the Caribbean, and probably couldn't find it on a map. This, in its way, was an
oblique homage to other bands I remember listening to on
the wireless as a kid: Liverpool-born Macari and his Dutch

Serenaders and London-born Felix Mendelssohn and his Hawaiian ditto.

The plot – such as it is – of *The Last Days of the Empire* centres on the disappearance of singer Enrico Olmedo – real name Simon Carruthers – who, it emerges, has run away with a pair of acrobatic dancers, the Janacek Sisters.

'Poor lad won't know which way to turn,' comments the bass player.

A replacement singer arrives from London. He is black and he announces himself thus: 'My name's Joe and I just got here from the Caribbean.' Calling him Joe was another homage – to the great Harriott, of course.

The serious theme buried inside the play was the way music, whether it's good or bad, tells us the truth about the people who make it. What the Gormans have written is not a genuine calypso but an innocent and well-intentioned rip-off – or, to express it in more high-flown language, an aspect of the cultural imperialism that goes in the wake of the political variety. In jazz terms it can be wrapped up in the question: who has a right to sing the blues? To which the democratic answer has to be: anybody who wants to, providing he or she is prepared to take on the audience.

I wrote lyrics for three songs in the show: a rousing chorus about the war, Mike and Peggy Gorman's old signature tune, and, of course, the calypso, which went something like this:

> It was such a grand celebration
> The day of the Queen's coronation
> It was such a grand celebration
> The day of the Queen's coronation
> The sun it shone bright

And I promised not to get tight
Grandma, the missus, the kids and me
On June the 2nd 1953
We went down to Westminster Abbey
Feeling so merry and happy
We went down to Westminster Abbey
Feeling so merry and happy
Then out came the Queen
She was looking sweet and serene
And oh what a happy day
God save the Queen and hip hip hooray.

We had to decide on someone to set music to this stuff and Jill Fraser, who runs the Watermill, said: 'You know John Dankworth. Why don't you ask him?'

The honest answer was I'd never thought of it. Besides, John was usually circumnavigating the globe with Cleo and even when at home, he was invariably juggling a dozen or more projects at any given time. But we asked him and to our delight he said yes.

It was a tricky assignment. These were supposed to be good bad songs, an affectionate pastiche of the sort of thing you would have heard in that fag-end period of variety theatre. The irony of the period, and of the play, was that the Coronation in 1953 – when millions of people watched television for the first time – caused the closure of more theatres than any other event, before or since. Even Hitler couldn't do it, certainly not on a permanent basis. It meant that Mike and Peggy's hit song was, in its way, a celebration of their own downfall.

This being a play, disaster piles up on disaster. Though they're playing twice-nightly, the first house is cancelled for total lack of an audience, and they then discover the theatre is to close after the second performance. It becomes, literally, the last day of the Empire.

The whole piece is, of course, a metaphor for the disintegration of the British Empire and the need to redefine our ideas about nations and nationality, using music as a way into the debate. It's also a lament for the great tradition of music-hall, buried under the successive tidal waves of the cinema, radio and television: three strikes and it was out. For the first half of the twentieth century it presented a big, colourful self-portrait of the nation and if, by the fifties, the picture had become a little shabby and dog-eared at the edges, there was genuine nobility in people like the Gormans, who carried on fighting to the end.

There's an old saying that travel broadens the mind, but the converse is also true. Broadening the mind can often have a dramatic effect on your forward travel arrangements.

All that is a fancy way of explaining how reading books led me to a collaboration with the Master of the Queen's Music. Or should that be Musick? It feels as if it should be.

The books I read were the stories and poems of George Mackay Brown, a great and totally unique Orcadian writer. He wrote exclusively about the Orkneys, the group of islands found across the Pentland Firth, north of John O'Groats in Scotland. You can see them on the weather map, but most days they are hidden by rain and beset by high winds.

We made our first visit in the early 1990s and it was love at first sight. The islands are not pretty. They are low-lying, like green basking whales. They are northern European in character and, at one stage, belonged to Norway. The gentle accent – described by George as 'like waves lapping in a pool' – is Norse in origin rather than Scottish. The history is ancient, with burial chambers five thousand years old, and signs of settlements even earlier. In Orcadian terms, Christ is a new kid on the block, spiritually speaking.

I had to write about all this but initially took the easy way out, by hiding inside somebody else's work. I dramatised George's novel, *Greenvoe*, for Channel 4. It's a strange, haunted but prescient story about the environment and how, when principalities and powers decide they want to exploit the land for their own dubious purposes, there's very little the commonfolk can do about it; except, in a little coda, George offers a message of hope that the people sometimes win in the end, though it might take a generation or two.

Unfortunately I delivered my scripts around the same time that Channel 4 was changing its chief executive. He, eager to prove his fitness for high office, sacked a number of people, including the Head of Drama who had commissioned my work. The project was apparently dead in the water, but for once the high level game of musical chairs became a blessing in disguise.

By now we had valuable contacts and friends in the islands and they suggested I do a version of *Greenvoe* as a community play, to form part of the annual St Magnus Festival, originally founded by George Mackay Brown and Peter Maxwell Davies and now a major international celebration of music and the arts.

Our community production of *Greenvoe* was presented at the festival in 2000 and later taken to Edinburgh where it played to packed houses and, famously, the critic from the *New York Times* couldn't get a seat. But it was in the Festival Club in Kirkwall, after the final performance of *Greenvoe*, that one of the actors said, in a scrupulously polite Orcadian manner: 'Now Alan, is it possible that you might consider writing us another play some time? Maybe an original piece of your own?'

It may have been the single malt talking, but I started to improvise a story, about a young Orcadian lass who might, or might not, have fallen in love with an Italian prisoner-of-war. That was about it, though I probably mentioned that music would play a part and I certainly suggested a title: *Barriers*.

The relationship between the islands and Italy is a heartening example of the transcendent power of art. It began with the sinking of the battleship, *Royal Oak*, on October 14th 1939 by a German submarine which found its way into Scapa Flow. Churchill ordered that barriers be built, linking the islands but also cutting off access by hostile intruders. Seven hundred Italian prisoners-of-war arrived in Orkney to assist with the work. There was an initial period of mutual hostility, but after a while they became part of the island landscape and, once Italy had swopped sides, part of the community too. They left behind a small gem of a chapel, transformed from Nissen huts under the guidance of a remarkable artist called Domenico Chiochetti, and links have remained to this day between his family and Orkney.

In the weeks and months that followed my conversation in the bar, the Festival organisers called my bluff. Was I serious? And when could I deliver *Barriers*? Then there was another phone call: 'Max wonders whether you'd mind if he wrote the music?'

I called Alexandra: 'Sir Peter Maxwell Davies, one of the world's greatest composers, wants to write the music for my play. It's obviously a compromise but sometimes it's inevitable. I think it would be churlish to refuse, don't you?'

Barriers is purely a work of the imagination, subtitled

Grandma's Saga, because it is the experience of the war years as she tells it; and since she is an imaginary character, we are two clear steps removed from a documentary record. What I tried to define was the emotional heartbeat of the period – not so much what happened, as what it felt like for the people involved within the three communities: the Orcadians, the Italians and the military. In particular, why this special relationship between Orkney and the Italians? I was reminded while writing it that Italian prisoners-of-war built prefabs a short walk from where I lived as a boy in Hull, but I'm not sure anyone remembers this now. But then, they didn't leave a chapel behind.

As with the John Dankworth connection, Max's contribution was not too onerous. He wrote three pieces: a military march to accompany traditional rude army lyrics about Bloody Orkney; some traditional-style Orkney fiddle music; and a setting for some Italian words written by Chiochetti himself. Compared with writing a full-scale opera or symphony it was, I suspect, a relatively easy gig. I can illustrate this. He and I were having lunch in Kirkwall to discuss the play when he suddenly started to scribble on the back of a menu.

'You've just written one, haven't you?' I said.

'Yes,' he said.

There's another tradition at the St Magnus Festival. If the writer is present he is expected to take a curtain call and say a few words. On the first night of *Barriers* I thanked the brilliant director, Penny Aberdein, and our wonderfully dedicated and talented cast. The National Theatre sent a spy to see the play in Edinburgh and he commented: 'We couldn't find actors this good. They couldn't handle the accent and they couldn't climb inside that culture.'

In my speech I thanked Max for his music and went on

to say:

'It's good to give a local composer a helping hand and I hope it leads on to even greater things in his career.'

About a year later he was made Master of the Queen's Music. I wrote to him and reminded him of my prediction. He replied, saying thank you. It proves that it's possible to be a world-renowned composer, a knight of the realm, Master of the Queen's Music, Musick, or possibly both, and, at the same time, a sweet guy and a very dear friend.

Gilbert and Sullivan and Barnes

These words are a triple homage, to G & S (in many ways
the precursors of the twentieth century popular song or any
rate the brand that assumes the presence of brain cells in
the listener) and to my writing partner of recent years, Alan
Barnes.

He is the very model of a modern jazz saxophonist
He knows the riffs and changes of the tunes they all play oftenist
He knows the standard variations sweet and sour and savoury
He plays them very fast indeed all demi-semi-quavery
At Open University he studied musicology
And for a bet he'll whistle Charlie Parker's Anthropology
He practises arpeggios that Dexter Gordon's fingers made
He goes to sleep while singing weird music Charlie Mingus made
And in his dreams he's always hanging cool man with the jazz elite
At Minton's and at Birdland and the dives on Forty-Second Street
And while his mother thinks he's just a layabout cacaphonist
He is the very model of a modern jazz saxophonist

When times are bad he's not too proud to play a little Dixieland
He's even played in pantomime – Red Riding Hood in Pixieland
He's dressed in funny clothes and done his share of low-brow
drollery
And even once wore a disguise to play some rock-and-rollery
He's doubled flute and oboe backing Miss Saigon at Drury Lane
And almost got a job as dep at Wavendon for Cleo Laine
He made the headlines in the papers when he paid a ten pound
fine
For playing flattened fifths while busking Stardust on the
Northern Line
But still he dreams of stardom and of being on the pull again

With groupies all beguiled by clever quotes from Gerry Mulligan
And while this week he's working as a chatline gay telephonist
He's still the very model of a modern jazz saxophonist

9.

Songs for Unsung Heroes

I realise this book has turned, willy nilly, into a kind of autobiography. I didn't mean it to, but, as is clear from many of the events described, my career is littered with things I didn't mean to do but turned out nice in the end.

When asked if I'd ever write a conventional autobiography, I've always said, very firmly, absolutely not. The reasons are very simple. What comes out is either a catalogue of alternating triumphs and disasters ('and then I wrote' repeated three hundred times) or a warts-and-all confessional, of the sort John Osborne wrote, brilliantly and ruthlessly. While I've probably got the average number of warts, I'm not particularly eager to brandish them in public, and they're really no more interesting than anybody else's warts.

Apart from that – and this is going to sound unbearably coy but it's true – I'm not sufficiently interested in my own psyche to spend 300 pages analysing it, and can't see any compelling reason to inflict thousands of words of self-analysis on a public that never asked for it in the first place. Jokes are much better value.

Peggy Ramsay used to say my modesty was my worst fault though a producer once said, with an alarming degree of accuracy: 'Alan is unrelentingly nice but you then realise with a bit of a shock that he generally gets his own way about everything that matters.'

Who knows? Maybe inside every modest playwright there's a devious bastard hoping not to be caught out.

It's very clear that looking back over seventy years, many of the key punctuation marks are musical: from hearing 'Mood Indigo' in my grandma's house in Jarrow to writing song cycles about the jazz heroes who have given some joy, shape and meaning to my life.

Music illuminates the writing process. I do occasional bouts of teaching, always on the understanding that writing cannot be taught, but a good teacher can help the apprentice to learn a little more quickly. One of the methods is to play a piece of music to the students with the challenge: 'Name the trumpet player.'

Invariably within four bars one of them will come up with the answer: 'Miles Davis.'

The lesson I draw from this runs:

'Consider what that man is doing. He is blowing through a mouthpiece into a piece of bent metal equipped with valves. There are thousands of these things in the world yet this man plays half-a-dozen notes and we know who he is. That's the challenge to the writer. That's how we recognise Shakespeare, Ibsen, Chekhov, Arthur Miller. It's your job to sound like yourself. Nothing more, nothing less. Sound like yourself and everything else will follow.'

Forget all the awards and the critical acclaim. Just about the finest compliment I was ever paid was at a football match in Hull in the 1960s when one of the supporters said to me: 'I enjoyed your *Z Cars* the other night. I could tell it was one of yours.'

My most recent stage play, *Sweet William*, illustrates the point that forty years on, I still sound like me, but with a few more wrinkles. Written for Barrie Rutter's sparkling Halifax-based Northern Broadsides company, the play is about Shakespeare having a night's drinking with his low companions down at the Boar's Head. Obviously I'm not the first writer to have a whack at depicting Our Founder and I won't be the last; but not too many would elect to open the piece with the entire company performing an Elizabethan rap:

> He's a card
> He's a one
> He's a bard
> He's a swan
> He can sing
> He's a king
> He's Wee Willy Shaggers from Stratford Town
> He can laugh
> He can cry
> He can chaff
> He can sigh
> He can weep
> In his sleep
> He's Wee Willy Shaggers from Stratford Town
> He's a scamp
> He's a scrote
> He's a tramp
> He's a goat
> He's a sod
> He's a god
> He's Wee Willy Shaggers from Stratford Town.

Dramatically the song has at least two primary functions. First, it tells the audience they're in for a loud and rumbustious night out, and though there's a dying fall at the end, that comes as a surprise. Second, it indicates that within the assembly of characters, there are divided opinions about our hero.

Footnote: the word 'scrote' doesn't appear in my *Chambers Dictionary*, nor in the 'Penguin Historical Slang' equivalent, though it is used in the North of England and in the work of the great Reginald Hill.

The music for *Sweet William* was written by Conrad Nelson, who also played Shakespeare. He's a gifted and versatile guy, who also provided memorable themes for an Elizabethan blues: an elegiac number about the virtues of strong drink; a rude song about the loss of virginity; and the best setting I've ever heard of Shakespeare's 'When that I was and a little tiny boy' from *Twelfth Night*, which I looted for the ending.

If the central challenge of writing is to sound like yourself, as simply and surely as Miles Davis, Johnny Hodges or Thelonious Monk, the secondary challenge is how to tell your story.

This raises the sometimes deadly subject of dramatic structure, about which thousands of words have been written, heavily laden with jargon like 'character arcs' and 'turning points' and seasoned with 'paradigms'. There are people who travel the world, preaching about this. Most of them are from Los Angeles, which is no surprise. I once suggested in an article that they are snake oil salesmen and one of them responded by saying that if we ever meet, he'll invite me to step outside. That's no problem. I won't go, though I might send a large and loyal friend, if there's one handy.

I'm only human and therefore not without faults but at least I don't stink up the place with arcs and paradigms. My approach to dramatic structure is to play Duke Ellington's 1940 version of 'Harlem Air Shaft' which contains all you need to know about dramatic structure, if you have ears to listen.

Armed with this slender syllabus – Miles Davis and Duke Ellington – I've travelled the world, disguised as a teacher. For the most part I don't remember much about the teaching, but I do remember the musicians we heard: a young James Morrison in Sydney, Louis Stewart in Dublin, Joanne Brackeen in Toronto, McCoy Tyner in Boston.

One of my proudest evenings, and this is a true anorak's confession, was in Stockholm. I was doing a last-minute rewrite on a thriller – an Anglo-American-Swedish co-production, which is an iffy start, and eventually a lousy movie, I'm told, which I've never been allowed to see. One of the Swedish producers invited me round to his house for supper. Knowing of my passion he had lined up some music to eat and drink by – especially to drink by, this being Scandinavia – and the implied challenge was to name the musicians. They were, naturally, the local heroes: Lars Gullin, Arne Domnérus, Bengt Hallberg. I scored a hundred per cent. At any rate, that's the way I remember it, to the extent that I remember anything at all about the evening.

In the midst of these globe-trolling adventures – slotted between the research trip to Jamaica for the Lenny Henry series that never happened and a teaching stint in Ottawa – we visited New Orleans. It made geographical sense, since from a European perspective, Ottawa, New Orleans and Jamaica are all more or less in the same street. The message to friends was we were taking a journey to Mecca so that I could touch the hem of history.

As the plane was flying in I said to Shirley:

'Guess what I can see.'

'What can you see?'

'The Mississippi Delta.'

Not just any old delta but Mark Twain's and King Oliver's. It was a moment to stir the soul; but as often happens, the sanctity was subverted by the echo of a cute joke.

It wasn't one of mine, but a memory of fellow jazz freak, Geordie-in-exile and Humberside-based broadcaster, Peter Adamson, saying: 'If all you need to invent jazz is a delta port with a multi-racial population, why didn't it happen in Goole?'

We discovered the answer as a result of trying to buy Kleenex in a vast shopping mall, about the size of Northumberland, at the top of Canal Street. It turned out that nobody sold Kleenex anywhere in the complex but during the search we stumbled by chance across the headquarters of the Louis Armstrong Foundation.

It emerged that the Foundation ran conducted tours of historical landmarks in the area and we ended up taking the trip on a Saturday afternoon – just the two of us, with the Foundation's director driving the van. I didn't tell him about the Port of Hull Jazz Band at the youth club raising my consciousness in 1951, or about Les and Barry and our trio and the misplaced bridge on my guitar.

It seemed irrelevant as he showed us the bayou and the levee, the odd remaining fragment of Storyville, the houses where Jelly Roll Morton and Sidney Bechet lived, the doorstep where Buddy Bolden sat and practised – next door to Nick La Rocca. The tour was supposed to last a couple of hours. We toured and talked for almost five. I didn't mention the delta port of Goole but I did put the question: 'Why did it happen here in New Orleans?'

The reply ran:

'Jazz began in New Orleans because the French had a different attitude to black slaves from that of the English and the Spanish. The French encouraged the slaves to preserve their tribal culture. I guess they also figured that happy slaves would work harder.'

'Not like the English,' I said. 'We like our slaves to be little Englishmen. Play cricket. Pass the port in the right direction. Read Trollope. Think of the Empire.'

'You said it, not me. Also the French encouraged intermarriage. Hence the Creole tradition.'

'Bechet.'

'Right.'

'So if you're going to be exploited by wicked imperialists, you recommend the French?'

'I guess. They've all been to New Orleans. The French, the English, the Americans.'

That was our abiding impression of New Orleans: it was very much its own place – not quite American, or African, or European, or Caribbean – but a genuine fusion, with contrasting cultures relishing each other's differences. They have a special way with language, including the pronunciation of the place name itself, which generally comes out as 'Nawlins' with a slight emphasis and a Johnny Hodges-style upward slur on the first syllable. But this isn't gospel; I have a concert recording of Fats Domino where he sings 'Walking to New Orleans' and the word comes out pure French. That's the glory of language; it never keeps still and helps playwrights stay in business.

The music – and this was 1992 – was disappointing. We heard a nice band led by trumpet player Wallace

Davenport, some touching and elegant morsels at Preservation Hall and a deal of dross. I mentioned bands like the Dirty Dozen or players like the Marsalis brothers and got a cool response: anyone playing a flattened fifth was, we felt, likely to be run out of town.

One very cold, very wet night, we found ourselves as virtually the only customers in a bar, listening to a genial but mediocre quintet. They asked if there was anything we'd like to hear.

Once we'd run through their Ellington repertoire, Shirley suggested 'Lover Man'. They'd never heard of it.

'Don't mention Charlie Parker,' I muttered, as we made our excuses and left. We walked back to the hotel through the pouring rain.

We resisted the various temptations on offer: the transvestite strippers, the mud wrestling, the tee-shirts decorated with resolutely funny slogans, the Dukes of Dixieland playing 'The Saints'. A street-wise kid and apprentice hustler conned a dollar out of us with a very old joke. A sharp-suited dude outside a clip joint said: 'Hey man, you've got a beautiful daughter.'

We laughed and declined his invitation to be clipped by his joint. We had perfected a range of responses by this time, ranging from: 'We're giving up tranvestite strip shows for Lent,' to: 'Mud wrestling? We can get all that at home.'

We relished these exchanges and always ended up laughing. And despite the tawdriness, and the wall-to-wall rip-off syndrome, precious gems remained: a unique area of architectural magic in the French Quarter, a sense of history you can touch and, even in the most cliché-ridden of the music, a plaintive echo of something Buddy Bolden once played.

To be sure, this is a romantic view but loving jazz has nothing to do with common-sense, focus groups or anyone's national curriculum, and everything to do with the stuff that dreams are made on.

Hurricane Katrina changed everything. The pictures we saw on television were heart-breaking and it's perversely poignant that a ghastly event be given such a pretty name. What the disaster, and its aftermath, revealed was what we all suspected: that underneath the beguiling exterior, New Orleans was home to as much poverty and deprivation as many a city in the third world. The simple statistic – that in the land of plenty here was a city where a hundred thousand people depended on public transport – gave many of us a chance to gloat about the George Bush version of democracy which he's so anxious to export to other parts of the planet.

There was another story at the time, grotesquely under-reported. Apparently Cuba, when it faced a similar threat, successfully evacuated over a million people and emerged with only a handful of casualties. This may be an invidious comparison but what happened in New Orleans means that awkward questions have to be asked, and if the answers are painful, that's the price a nation pays for looking in the other direction for a century or more.

For those of us living in the relative security of the United Kingdom, the overall feeling was and is one of helplessness and frustration. Music lovers can do their bit. Ronnie Scott's organised a major fund-raiser to help musicians in the city and we were all happy to join in; but ultimately the response has to be bigger than that and – whether we like it or not – it has to be entrusted to the politicians, both regional and national.

As for the big question – what should be done with the city of New Orleans? – the answer is very simple. Ask the people who live there. It's time they had a proper say in their own destiny, even if it's a little late in the day.

There are millions of ways of interpreting the world and trying to make sense of it, but writing plays is the one I've ended up with. Similarly, there are millions of ways of interpreting plays, but one persuasive idea that keeps bubbling up in my head is that every play is a love letter: to an individual, or a group, or an entire community – perhaps real, perhaps imaginary, perhaps dwelling in a parallel universe halfway between.

Alan Barnes and I started writing musical love letters to a motley selection of heroes about five years ago. I suspect our first inspiration was Lily Goodman from Cannon Hill in Birmingham. She was a seventeen-year-old amateur dancer who, on April 2nd and 3rd, 1923, at the Palais de Danse, Monument Road, Ladywood, danced non-stop for twenty-four hours and five minutes. This broke the British record for marathon dancing. She covered just over 68 miles, used up two partners – Mr R Webster-Grinling and Mr Harold Quiney – and 482 tunes. Lily received her prize from the champion jockey, Steve Donoghue.

Nobody knows what any of the tunes were so Alan wrote an instrumental in her honour as part of a programme called *Swinging Down Broad Street* for the Birmingham Jazz Festival in 2001. I was given the task of introducing the numbers, telling the stories behind them and keeping the audience quiet at Ronnie's.

Over a friendly glass of dandelion and burdock, Alan and I agreed it would be fun to write some songs about people like Lily: essentially people who had never had songs written about them. *Songs for Unsung Heroes* was the result and

ESSENCE OF BARNES

had we bothered with a mission statement it would have gone something like this:

'We want to write songs for the kind of people, places and institutions usually neglected by song-writers – for wonderful musicians like Joe Harriott and Sonny Criss – for great originals like Slim Gaillard and Spike Milligan – for local rhythm sections, jazz anoraks, RAC route maps and slobs who don't wash as often as they might.'

Since then we've done occasional live performances and made a CD with the sublime Liz Fletcher, backed by Alan's all-star band. I sometimes introduce them as his Clouds of Joy, if I remember. The mission statement continues:

'On the night, Alan Plater introduces the songs and tells the stories behind them. Imagine going to see *The Marriage of Figaro* and finding Mozart leading the band on reeds and Lorenzo Da Ponte explaining the jokes and you get the idea.'

Among the subjects clamouring for attention in the next extravanganza, *Seven Ages of Jazz*, are the Original Dixieland Jazz Band, Nat Gonella, Zoot Sims, blues for people who don't deserve them, and the shipping forecast areas. The mission statement concludes:

'There are millions of people, places and institutions on the planet Earth and all of them deserve songs. We hope they will form an orderly queue.'

To end at the beginning. . .

Duke Ellington said 'I must have music every day.'

I know the feeling.

This is not a book of intimate confessions, but here are a couple. Whenever a great jazz musician dies, we play his or her music in the house.

And each time a new grandchild arrives, or young friends have a baby, we play the Thad Jones/Mel Lewis recording of 'A Child is Born', and we cry with joy.

The message is as simple as the blues itself: in good times or bad, we must embrace the beauty.

AND FINALLY...

A by A.

Closing Credits

I thank my publishers, Ann and Roger Cotterrell a) because they only publish books that I want to read and b) for having the geographical sensitivity to live a short walk from where I live – and believe me, such a walk has to be really short to qualify.

I also thank a friend from the distant past, Mike Brumhead, who sent me the only surviving photograph of me with my guitar, and his late brother Les with his zither, all now revealed to the world on the back cover. Also in the picture are Bill (banjo) and an unknown clarinet player, possibly a kid called Pete. We couldn't play any of the instruments.

Years before he wrote and directed the marvellous movie, 'Brassed Off', Mark Herman did the drawing on the front cover. At the time Mark thought it also looked a bit like Alan Ayckbourn but has given his permission to use it here, because I was the first to ask.

I did all the other drawings and they appear with my permission.

My wife, Shirley, keeps a gentle and loving eye on my spelling, grammar, punctuation, table manners and life.

The song lyrics are from the CDs, *Songs for Unseen Heroes* and *Seven Ages of Jazz*, which is due for release in the spring of 2006 – all music written by Alan Barnes, played by his all-stars, with the luminous Liz Fletcher singing the songs. Both are on Woodville Records, and available from the usual sources: music stores, car boot sales, dodgy geezers on the Holloway Road or try a direct approach to the composers.

The final thank you is to all the musicians in all the bands in all the gin joints in all the world, without whom...

Alan Plater
20 November 2005

Other Books from Northway

Ronnie Scott with Mike Hennessey
Some of My Best Friends Are Blues

Alan Robertson
Joe Harriott – Fire in His Soul

Coleridge Goode and Roger Cotterrell
Bass Lines: A Life in Jazz

Peter Vacher
Soloists and Sidemen: American Jazz Stories

Harry Gold
Gold, Doubloons and Pieces of Eight

Digby Fairweather
Notes from a Jazz Life

Jim Godbolt
A History of Jazz in Britain 1919-50

Ron Brown with Digby Fairweather
Nat Gonella – A Life in Jazz

Northway Publications, 39 Tytherton Road, London N19 4PZ, info@northwaybooks.com